WRITE YOUR WAY TO SUCCESS
with the Paragraph System

Caulean Vesey

EXCEL PRESS
Box 123 Riverdale, New Jersey 07457

Library of Congress Publication Data

    Vesey, Caulean
      WRITE YOUR WAY TO SUCCESS
    with the Paragraph System

    Excel Press
    TXU 75-378 1980   82-08312
    ISBN 0-9609582-0-7 pbk.

Production Data

    Typesetting/design by Vera Caras
    Cover by Hanna Ericson

© 1981 by Caulean Vesey

*T*his book
was created
to meet a basic
educational need:

students have a right to
the facts of writing.

Contents

I

THE PARAGRAPH SYSTEM

Chapter 1

Your Presentation $\quad$ 3

Chapter 2

Reading Paragraph Plans $\quad$ 9

II

WRITE YOUR WAY TO SUCCESS

Acknowledgments

*T*his work is dedicated to my teacher, Margaret Henderson.

I also wish to acknowledge the help of Beth Leventhal, Deena Delzengoff, Marilyn Hirsh, Jodi Sanders, Paul Antonelli, Jill Shultz, Ronnie Feierstein, John Madero, Helen Cutler, John Cito, Phil Fier, Irving Felsher, and Arthur Forrest. ■

Preface

I wanted a *system* for teaching writing. I wanted my system to guarantee success for every student who would conscientiously put the principles into practice. To satisfy my goal I developed a method of learning how to write through plans and models. Then, after years of classroom testing, I wrote it up as *WRITE YOUR WAY TO SUCCESS with The Paragraph System.*

My teaching friends liked the system. They wanted *WRITE YOUR WAY TO SUCCESS* to become a book for teachers to use with their classes.

My parent friends also liked the system. They wanted a book that could show them how to give their children writing security. They wanted a book that could show them how to give solid — but, strictly practical — writing direction for all the school-related composition assignments their children would be required to write.

My students liked the system. They wanted a book that could show them how to learn on their own. They also wanted a system that would be respected by all teachers, and one that could insure they could get top grades.

And, although the objectives of each of these groups seem to be different, and they might even seem to exclude one another, they are — to my way of thinking — identical: moreover, they do not exclude each other.

Isn't it one of the tragic facts of American education that there has never been a single published book that meets these important and collective needs.

That's why I wrote *WRITE YOUR WAY TO SUCCESS with the Paragraph System*. And, that's why it's organized the way it is. So, don't skip around. Go step by step. Make it your goal to do each exercise until you know it by heart. Above all, remember that this is not a book you read; it's a book you *write*.

For those who are interested in the unusual chain of events that led me to the paragraph system and to writing this book, you will find the story in the *Introduction*. But let me begin on an equal footing with all teachers, parents, and students by simply speaking to you as . . .   ■

Introduction

$\mathcal{D}$ear Friends,

Was I bewildered!

Every September I used to face the same frustration that most teachers of English face: the students couldn't really read; they couldn't write; they couldn't follow simple verbal instructions.

Yet, these same students were serious about school and about the kind of education they wanted. Often they came to me in private to ask what they could do to help themselves, and these were the problems about which they most frequently spoke: how to get placed in classes where the students were more conscientious; how to get better grades in English, and how to get better grades in all courses with written tests. And a few brave kids would hit the center of the problem when they asked point-blank if I could please teach them how to write.

And every September I was stunned by the irony that the writing problem wasn't getting better: it was getting worse!

How could I help these deserving kids? How could I help the equally deserving ones who didn't have the nerve to ask? We had experienced a constant decline in reading scores and an accompanying decline in writing skills. To my way of thinking we were swamped with language-failure. However, yesterday's textbooks were worthless for bringing my students' language proficiency up to a literacy level necessary for learning.

I had, though, glimpsed a solution from my past experiments with a teaching technique I had developed and had come to call *patterning*. So, I set out to combine the most successful of these experiments into a developmental program to overcome language-failure through writing. After three years, further experimentation on some 500 students, 100,000 written words, I had structured a functional system for learning how to write; it was built on two sets of essentials: the first set, an index of paragraphs, provided a visual plan to show how the paragraph was organized, and a written model to show the language; the second set, an index of compositions, each with a visual-plan-outline, showed how to link the paragraphs together into coherent projects, and showed the student how to write whatever future compositions that would be required in English and all the other subjects as well.

On the first day I presented a class with a paragraph plan which I had drawn on the blackboard, and then dictated the matching word model, the students saw that they had the chance to get some control — a secure handle — on their grades. They soon called my program "write-your-way-to-success-with-Vesey's-paragraph-system." And they proceeded to do exactly that! But with this bonus: they loved it!

Here's how the kids did it: they learned the paragraphs one at a time by copying the plans and models. Then, they would pattern their composition to the plan and model. It was a lot like having a private teacher there at their sides during homework time. Of equal importance, these compositions were most often based on the reading assignments. This meant that the students were never at a loss for something to write about.

When they advanced to longer compositions — mostly reports because that is what every student needs to know how to do to succeed in school or to succeed in the business world—they gained an even deeper learning experience. Here, they read from the class literature book or novel, but they also added to their experience by drawing from a broad range of library materials; moreover, they took pages of notes — which, incidentally, became increasingly accurate as the year progressed. Through the paragraph sets they came to examine their lives and life in their community, and to examine their own thoughts. They wrote and read their compositions in class and discussed the writing and then wrote again. With this new reading-based approach to composition, the patterning philosphy smoothly traveled from whatever the students read into whatever they wrote: the standardized sentence structure, vocabulary, grammar, usage, spelling, and punctuation crept from the printed page into the students' script. They were quick to see how they had gained control over their learning. That first test class experienced an average gain of fifteen points on their report card average and a two-point-nine jump on their reading scores.

Since then, all my students in all my classes have shown an unprecedented all-scores and all-skills improvement whether they came to me in Spetember reading four years below-level or four years above.

What makes WRITE YOUR WAY TO SUCCESS with the

Paragraph System so unusual?

The plans for the paragraphs speak for themselves: one look, and the students instantly know how to organize the paragraph. Similarly, the frames provide the perfect map for writing longer compositions.

Too, conceptual models have always been the best writing teachers: for generations students and professionals alike have shaped their work on such models as the Bible, Shakespeare, and Hemingway, to name a few.

However, the paragraph models in *WRITE YOUR WAY TO SUCCESS* perform a more intimate, a more specific or detailed function: when the students make their initial copy, the plans and models seem to form a firm pattern in their memories; and, then, when they create their own paragraphs, they unconsciously approximate the organization, but the wording, of course, is entirely their own.

WRITE YOUR WAY also provides some powerful benefits:

First, and most importantly, the students greatly improve their reading skills. Reading with note-taking is essential if the students are going to come into class properly prepared: note-taking provides them with their only concrete account of the details; note-taking is the only way they can control their memory and comprehension without guessing; and note-taking eliminates the boredom and mind-meandering by converting reading from a passive to an active process.

Moreover, *WRITE YOUR WAY* makes for superb public relations: parents can see their children's success. They also see that their kids are leaning useful material that they never had the opportunity to learn. They see, too, that a seventh grader trained in the *WRITE YOUR WAY* program can often out-write adults, even those with college degrees.

More importantly, however, *WRITE YOUR WAY* brings

equal-rights to every English class where it is used. Unlike math where the students are shown a formula and then shown how to do the problem correctly, in English we have foolishly required the students to discover formulas and solutions to writing problems on their own. This discovery-gamble has made English an easy mark for the advantaged few while the disadvantaged many withdraw, sinking into the protection of silence. With *WRITE YOUR WAY* all the students have open-access to writing organization and models; they all have open-access to concrete informtion and potential content for their compositions; and they have open-access to organizational control over their ideas and words. Further, they all have open-access to the mainstream of American English and to all the mechanical details of writing. Isn't that what they must have to succeed in every level of academic life? Isn't that what they must have to succeed in the business world? And, it is this unique and revolutionary approach that has brought equal-opportunity out of the courtroom and into the classroom where it belongs!

Too, no student need be held back by the textbook, by the teacher, by the pace of the class, by the atmosphere of the school, by the pressure of the community, or by the family's social class. When students see the progressively improving quality and maturity of their writing, they dare to reach out further: they self-teach as they branch into topics that capture their imagination; they specialize; they accelerate; they build solid expertise; and they learn still more by teaching others what they've learned from *WRITE YOUR WAY TO SUCCESS* with the Paragraph System.

Now, my students who used to struggle against unfair placement write their way up to better classes. The kids who wanted so badly to excel in English write their way to excellence, not only in English but in every class where the grade is based on a written examination. As for the want-to-be-writers, they have formed a legion of students who have won or placed in essay contests where the number of competitors has run as high as 43,000. That's prize writing!

Writing is the only act that will cause the student to stop and to grapple with the word; with its spelling, meaning, and implications. Writing is the only proof of competent thought: the spoken word, after all, vanishes forever the instant after it is said. Writing is the only way to redirect the flood of language-failure. And, if we are serious about helping the students with language, *WRITE YOUR WAY TO SUCCESS with the Paragraph System* is the best way to show them how! ■

I

THE PARAGRAPH SYSTEM

1

Your Presentation

— Writing is Self-Expression —

*H*ave you ever wondered about script? Probably not. But you have asked yourself this question: "Does neatness count?"

You bet it does! In fact, neatness is *the* first impression your paper makes; moreover, the appearance of your composition is a lot like handing in a photograph of yourself. Of course, you'll say to yourself at this point, it would have to be the right kind of photograph with exactly the right background because you would want to control the kind of impression you'll make. Keep that ideal snapshot in mind because that is what you're going to want to get your script to do.

Make your heading count. Make it perfectly spaced; afterall, it is a statement of what you think of yourself and of your school.

Make your title count. Center it exactly.

Make every paragraph count: in practice this means that the closing section should be as carefully presented as the opening.

Make every word count: in practice this means that the first letter must begin with a capital or lower case letter, whichever is required. The words must be correctly spelled. To not dot an *i* or not cross a *t* is to spell the word incorrectly. However, no word can be correctly spelled if the writing is not perfectly neat because sloppy script conceals spelling errors.

Make every space count: in practice this means that the indentations at the beginning of each paragraph must be generous and uniform. Your left-hand margin must form a straight line; try to keep your right-hand margin an inch in from the paper's edge. Although it's not practical to force this margin into a straight line, you will want to keep it as attractive as possible.

Making every space count also means that the spaces for and next to commas, apostrophes, and dashes must be clear; and that end marks — periods, question marks and exclamation marks—must also have their clear place and appropriate space.

Make space between your paragraphs clear. When writing in paragraph sets — you'll learn more about this later — you'll begin a paragraph on the next line after you have finished one. However, there will be other times when you will want to skip lines between paragraphs.

Make your style count. Go for a no-nonsense, finely-tuned script. No flourishes! No nonstandard letters that could jolt your reader. No circles for dots and periods. If you have difficulty maintaining quality script for the length of a page or more, then change your time frames: write five lines, take a break, and then come back and write five more, and so on until your composition is finished.

Now is the time for you to make time to improve your script.

Copy the following sample on notebook paper. Draw the letters slowly and painstakingly. It will take time, but if you plan to achieve success through writing, you must do every step as well as you possibly can. Besides, fine script is well worth the effort. Learning the penmanship that makes for a good presentation is better than you running along with your papers and trying to explain what it is you meant to say. And, a fine presentation will make that important first impression that says your paper is a candidate for a top grade!

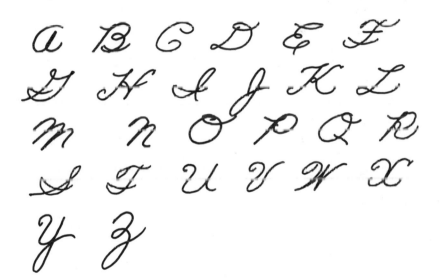

a b c d e f g
h i j k l m n
o p q r s t
u v w x y z

1 2 3 4 5 6 7 8 9 0

A B C D E F
G H I J K L
M N O P Q R
S T U V W X
Y Z

Your compositions
should always be written

on standard-ruled, 8 x 10½-inch loose-leaf paper with margin lines. Make the best presentation possible. This visible display of interest and skill is your personal endorsement of the content, development, and organization that you have put into your work. Moreover, the quality of your presentation is a reflexion on the quality of your teachers, your school, and your education; but more importantly, it is your statement of yourself!

Let your good presentation become a statement of your good thinking. You might recognize the faulty thinking in some of these familiar excuses often handed in with composition papers. I like to tell my students that I only accept papers, not excuses. I have added my private comments to these student protests.

"Neat handwriting is immature."

How can you knock success?

"You think this handwriting is bad? You should see my doctor's stuff."

That could be. You may fill out your application to medical school with whatever scramble-script you like; but, if you plan to file that application, I advise you to get top grades, and the only way you deserve top grades is to write in top quality script.

"I'm left-handed . . . "

I have yet to meet a left-handed student who wanted to do fine work and who failed to learn how.

"I can't!"

To me that translates to "I won't," or "you can't make me do anything I don't want to do." But very shortly after the beginning of the school year, students who think this way have a change of mind.

8

"You should see the way my parents write!"

Your parents may not have had the opportunity to get a good education. You have, and it's my responsibility to see that you do.

"Can I type mine?"

Typewritten homework is inappropriate. Typewritten compositions invite enormous questions. Who really wrote the paper? Who typed it? Who edited it as they went along? However, there are no solid answers to these questions. More importantly, using the typewriter as a solution for script problems doesn't solve the problem, it merely postpones it. Typewriters won't help you when you're called to write essay questions for tests, write in-class compositions, compete in college admissions, or write for license examinations.

Take charge of your education by developing the good script that will insure that your compositions make a good presentation.
Make a clear statement for your rights by making your presentations say that *you* have the right to a top grade.

— Writing is making your thoughts permanent —

2

Reading Paragraph Plans

— Writing is the management of words —

*N*o professional writer would waste time writing a piece without first laying out a good plan: building any piece of writing is a lot like building a house; if you don't have a good plan, you can't have control.

For the writer with less experience, good plans are even more important. Sentence plans — or patterns as they are called — won't work because they are not complete thoughts: however, if we fasten sentences together in their natural grouping, we will have a *paragraph,* and the paragraph will always perform as the ideal or perfect package for your thoughts.

Perhaps we can gain a better understanding of every paragraph if we stopped thinking of it as a paragraph and started thinking of it as a room in a house. A paragraph, afterall, is very much like a roon in a house: both rooms and paragraphs have entries or indentations; both have walls or margins; both perform special types of work; both have specific details; and, both are built on specific plans.

So that every student can begin the study of writing with the appropriate information, lets look at an empty paragraph plan.

The Paragraph Plan

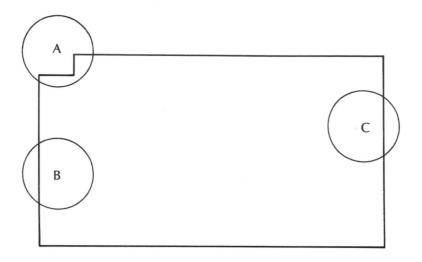

Now, to examine the plan: at the letter *A* we have the entry into the paragraph or the *indentation.* On the typewriter we usually count in five spaces and begin typing on the sixth, but when writing — in script as most of your work will be — the convenient method for spacing is the rule-of-thumb. Use your thumb for marking off the space from the left-hand margin to the beginning of the first word of your indentation. Use it for all your paragraphs to give your indentations a uniform look.

At letter *B* you will find a straight line descending or dropping from the indentation to the bottom line of the paragraph plan. This is called the left-hand margin line. You will want to make yours as straight as the one here. Make a point to always use loose-leaf paper with a left-hand margin printed in place.

Find letter C. This is the right-hand margin. On the plan it is shown as a straight line, but on your papers it will be irregular because you will have limited control over where your lines of writing are going to end: however, you can keep a neat and attractive distance from the right-hand edge of the paper by using your thumb.

If your paragraphs always follow this plan, making correct use of the instructions as shown in A, B, and C, then your paragraphs will always form a correct outline.

Fixed Details within the Paragraph Plan

Now that we understand the outline of the paragraph plan, let's take a look inside. Like the room in the house, the paragraph has *fixed* details or unmovable details. Examine the following plan:

Fixed Details

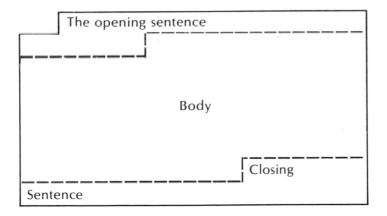

Every paragraph has an *opening sentence*. This sentence may be a statement, a question, or an exclamation. It may be of any length.

After the opening sentence we come to the *body* of the paragraph which may be any number of sentences.

The *closing sentence,* as shown in the plan, always comes at the paragraph's end.

Learning to read paragraph plans is necessary if you are going to be able to read the plans in this book. There are fourteen paragraph plans in this edition of *WRITE YOUR WAY TO SUCCESS with the Paragraph System.* They are the plans for the *Narration, Persuasion, the Zig-Zag, Description, Exposition, the Character Sketch, Comparisons, Comparisons and Contrasts, Contrast, Contrast Point-By-Point, Cause and Effect, Problem and Solution, Parallel Development,* and *the Before and After.*

You will also find your knowledge of paragraph plans useful in your reading: one, you will have a visual sense of how the paragraph is organized, and this will improve your comprehension; then two, when you read a paragraph where the style appeals to you or you find it particularly well-crafted, you can easily draw a plan of the passage for your own future use.

If some of the steps discussed in these first two chapters seemed too easy for you, then you are fortunate. Every student who wants to learn how to write hasn't necessarily picked up this information, and fortunately for them it was explained in the beginning. Remember too, this book promises to show you how to write your way to *success,* and *success* means *understanding* every step and *doing* every step exactly right!

— Writing is thinking —

3

Basic Paragraphs I

— Writing is the management of thought—

NARRATION

*T*he narrative, in plain talk, tells a story. The best way for you to control the telling of any story is through the use of *time-order connectives.*

Examine the following plan for these time-order connectives. Also, you will want to take careful note of the time-order connectives when you read the model for the narrative paragraph on the following page.

Plan for the Narrative Paragraph

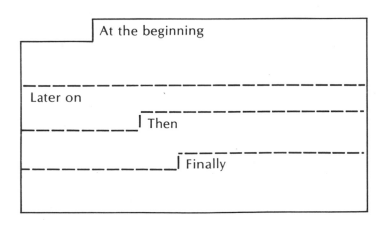

<u>Model for the Narrative Paragraph</u>

At the beginning of my first day of this school year, my head was filled with some hazy impressions. The building seemed impossibly large; in fact, so much so that I was afraid I would spend most of my time trying to find my way from one class to the next. As things turned out, I somehow made it to all my classes before the late bell. Later on, I found myself feeling as though I were totally alone because I didn't recognize any of the other students in any of my classes. Then, I found myself worrying about being able to do the homework. I couldn't believe the assignments! And, for every class! Finally, I was almost afraid to go home at the day's end, but not for any reasons that I understood at the time: the truth was I didn't want to wait eighteen long hours for the next day to begin.

As you have noticed, the narrative cannot take place in the blink-of-any-eye; instead, it must take place during a period of time. For that reason, time plays a special — and a highly visible role in the narrative. You were probably introduced to your first *time-order* connective when you heard the words, *once upon a time*. As your reading became more sophisticated, you were introduced to flashbacks. Perhaps you are already aware of time control through the use of day and night or the seasons of the year.

Another important quality of the narrative is that *something* happened. Moreover, the something happened to *someone*. And, all this took place *somewhere*.

Notice that word, *someone:* this presents you with a choice which you should make before you begin writing your narrative. You will want to decide what *voice* to use. If you are going to write about yourself, you most probably will choose the pronoun *I*, or as it is called technically, the voice of the first person. However, you might choose to write about someone else, and in that case you will use that person's name. This approach is called using the voice of the third person. It is rare that you will every tell a story using the voice of the second person, *you*.

There are numerous connectives with which you will want to familiarize yourself to help you write more effective narratives. Some of these are the following: first, next, then, eventually, since, meanwhile, in the meantime, later, afterward, finally, and in the end.

You might have already noticed that narrative writing offers many choices for subject material, voicing, and connectives. But have you also noticed that the narrative almost always takes place in the *past:* even if it takes place at the moment of writing, or in the future, it will still be written as though it had already happened or in the *past tense*.

Application of the Narrative

Whether your narratives are going to be nonfiction or fictionalized versions of some true story, you will usually find it helpful to build the writing of your narrative on some personal experience. The following list will provide you with some concepts that always make for enjoyable writing topics: the unforgettable moment, a camping trip, the picnic, a birthday party, a fishing trip, an accident or fire, gift giving, a family reunion, or finding your lost dog.

The Narrative as a Reading-Reporting Aid

The narrative has another — although unrecognized — and perhaps more important role: the narrative technique may be used to *summarize* reading assignments for every academic subject. For anyone who wants to be in control of their education, the summary is indispensable. The summary will become your only record of the reading; your most useful opportunity for a review of the material; and, should you need evidence that you did the assignment, your summary will become the written proof.

For the skilled writer, summaries are to be written with great care: any fictionalization, any shift in emphasis or in proportion, any departure from the original, is not only to incorrectly summarize the material, but it will also decrease your understanding of the work.

The summary then goes on to play a major role in the commercial world; here it is strictly exactness and any fictionalizing is reason enough for the writers to lose their jobs.

In the medical, scientific, or legal world the summary becomes even more demanding: here it is known as the *abstract*.

And, finally, at its most perfect level, the summary becomes the *precis:* the precis, by definition, means to be exact; and to write a precis means to — within the limitations of language — create a picture in miniature of another written work.

PERSUASION

The paragraph to persuade — also known as the paragraph to convince, the argument, argumentation, or the argumentative paragraph— is designed to help you *prove* a point.

In examining the following plan, note that this paragraph introduces a new concept, the *topic sentence.*

Plan for a Paragraph to Convince

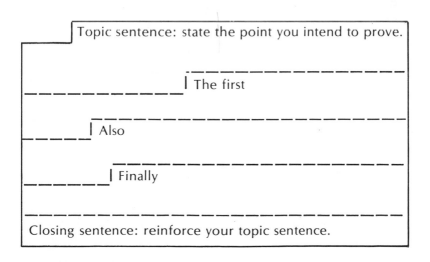

Topic sentence: state the point you intend to prove.

The first

Also

Finally

Closing sentence: reinforce your topic sentence.

Model for the Paragraph to Convince

Although many young people are willing to accept the tradition of being seated in the children's section of the theater when seeing a movie, I — for one — strongly object to such a practice. I say this for three reasons. The first, and certainly the least important, is that this seating system prevents me from taking the seat of my choice. Also, this system forces me to sit with others — kids, if you will — who do not necessarily know how to behave in a theater. Finally, I am being denied my money's worth because I am paying an adult price, but I am only getting a child's seat. In the future I intend to patronize only those theaters where, for my adult-priced-ticket, I can expect to be treated like an adult.

The details of the paragraph to persuade might be arranged in order of least importance, or in order of most importance; however they are arranged, it is for the convenience of the author and to convince the reader that the point being developed here is *true*. Announcing how many reasons are to be given allows the reader to keep tabs on what is being said. These connectives are also useful to the writer because they prevent the discussion from jumping off on a tangent.

If you want further supporting comments to any of your reasons, you can easily expand within a section without disturbing the organization of your paragraph.

Detail for Expanding a Reason

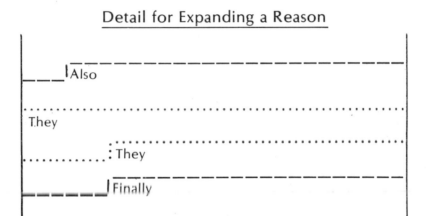

Model for Expanding a Reason

. . .*know how to behave in a theater. They can disrupt my concentration with their talk. They can easily spoil my entertainment with their slurping, crunching, munching, or tossing away whatever has not completed its destination into their little stomachs. Finally* . . .

Expanding on the basic paragraph is a useful technique. No matter how carefully you try to set up your original list of details to be included into your paragraph's first draft, you will often find—perhaps even days after you thought you had it all down in black-and-white — that there is some additional detail or set of details that you would like to insert to support a point or to clarify your paragraph.

Material can rarely be tacked on to a well-designed paragraph, but it can always — with any paragraph plan — be inserted into the paragraph.

In writing the paragraph to persuade you will have the opportunity to increase your understanding of connectives. Additional connectives you might use are the following: second, secondly, similarly, such as, since, thus, third, thirdly, then, accordingly, certainly, of course, moreover, however, and too.

As you become more experienced with the use of connectives and writing to persuade, you will discover that each connective is a separate and distinct tool which can bring measured degrees of leverage to your writing.

Good paragraphs to persuade come from the thoughtful development of one side of a controversial issue. If there are no widely divergent opinions on your topic, then you'll gain nothing worth the effort. Strength of language and daring — having the nerve to write what you believe — are necessary to success in persuasion. Apathy, decency, drugs, ecology, exploitation, greed, human rights, law-and-order, morality, politics, religion, rioting, and world events all provide an unending source for topics that will help you polish your powers of persuasion.

THE ZIG-ZAG

Imagine that you are finishing the opening paragraph of a short story in what you consider to be a high-quality magazine. Now, read an opening in your English book. Next, look at an opening for an article in the Sunday supplement of your local newspaper. Do they seem to all have something in common?

Well-designed opening paragraphs are similar: they are built in two parts; *the foundation,* and *the platform.* they are not difficult to write once you know the secret, and you'll want to know the secret because opening paragraphs have a lot to do with the kind of grades your papers will get.

The following opening is for a book report. This should prove especially useful because students write more book reports than any other type of composition. Note that the foundation is made of the question, the first connective, and your story; the platform is made of the second connective and theme sentence.

Plan for a Zig-Zag Paragraph

Question?	Connective
Your story	
	Connective
Theme sentence	

Model for a Zig-Zag Paragraph

Did you ever dream of hitting the perfect home run? I know I did! But my homer stayed in the dream-stage up until last summer, and oddly enough by that time I had nearly quit playing ball. Still, I found myself at the plate, and naturally I forgot about getting a hit because it was almost too dark to see the ball. I let the first pitch go by. I went after the second one with everything I had. By some coincidence my bat connected with one of those rare, solid smashes that sent a ringing "craaaack," through the dusky air and sent the ball soaring while I leisurely ran the bases to home. However, hitting homers is not easy, especially when you're desperate, and Casey — the desperate batter who needed a home run in Earnest Thayer's poem, "Casey at the Bat" — had an experience far less rewarding than mine.

How Does the Zig-Zag Work?

The Zig-Zag paragraph, as an opening for a book report, is as important for what it does as for what it says. Unlike other paragraphs where the words *tell*, here they *act* to hook the reader. In this case, the hook is the opening question.

The question technique takes the reader by surprise. It might be an embarrassing question such as, "Did you ever cheat on a test?" Or, a highly personal question such as, "Did you every seriously think about running away?" These "Do you . . .", "Have you . . .", or "Should you . . ." openings must relate, of course, in some important way to the poem, story, or book on which you are reporting.

Once you catch your readers' attention with that question, they will be more than willing to consider an answer. Here is where you come on: afterall, you are the author, you are calling the shots, and whose material do you know best? Your own! You're going to answer your question with your own story.

After your story has reached its conclusion your reader will accept a transfer — and connectives do that so smoothly — to the subject of your book report. But stepping from your foundation requires great care.

The connective linking your story with the goal of the Zig-Zag, the theme sentence, may be a single term such as *however* or *similarly,* or this second connective may be a short sentence. In any case, the theme sentences it introduces must be written with great care: this sentence will tell the character's name, title of the piece, type of literature, the author's name, and some easy hint of the theme. This theme sentence and its connective will provide a fine platform upon which you can construct an award-winning report.

Trouble-shooting the Question

It's simple to ask a good theme-related question, but be sincere about it and be sincere about the answer. Here's how other students have managed their openings.

On <u>Are</u> <u>You</u> <u>There</u> <u>God?</u> <u>It's</u> <u>Me,</u> <u>Margaret</u> by Judy Blume:

Have you ever wondered if anyone really listens to you? This question has worried me for the longest time .

On <u>Hamburger</u> <u>Heaven</u> by James Kenny:

How can anyone allow determination to rule their life? My friend Jean . . .

On <u>Lisa</u> <u>Bright</u> <u>and</u> <u>Dark</u> by John Neufeld.

Could a friend's failing mental health hurt you? I watched my Aunt Ellen nearly destroy my mother. Once a week Ellen . . .

On <u>The</u> <u>Red</u> <u>Pony</u> by John Steinbeck:

Were parents more interested in their children during the 30's than they are today? I can't answer that question from my own experience, but my grandparents told me . . .

On <u>Arriving</u> <u>at</u> <u>a</u> <u>Place</u> <u>You</u> <u>Never</u> <u>Left</u> by Lois Ruby:

Did you ever know anyone to fall head-over-heels in love? I did! My friend Julie met . . .

Approaching the Theme Sentence

Moving from the opening question, onto the first connective, and then through your narrative is not difficult; on the contrary, you'll find the zig-zagging unbelievably easy. However, moving out of your narrative and onto the second connective and then onto the theme sentence is not only more difficult, but it will require some real thinking on your part.

You may move from the foundation to the theme sentence in three different ways. The easiest way is to make a *direct* approach.

On approaching the theme sentence directly with a connective term:

. . .Similarly to my experience, Arthur, in The Stepmother, a short story by Margaret Jackson, also learned that real beauty lay in the eye of the beholder.

On approaching the theme sentence directly with a connective sentence:

. . . My experience was shocking but hardly unique. Arthur, in The Stepmother by Margaret Jackson, also learned that real beauty lay in the eye of the beholder.

Often though, you are going to find that your most interesting experiences are not necessarily similar to those found in the story, but that there is a relationship. In this case you will find the most effective approach to the theme sentence is to ease in on an angle or take what is known as the *oblique* approach.

On approaching the theme sentence obliquely with a connective term.

. . . My cousin needed only a year to adjust to her new parent. However, it took Arthur Steel, the star basketball player in Margaret Jackson's short story, <u>The Stepmother</u>, ten long years to make his choice.

On approaching the theme sentence obliquely with a connective sentence.

. . . My cousin needed a year to adjust to her new father. Other kids require a much longer period to make up their minds. For example, Arthur — also known as Stretch — Steel, star of Margaret Jackson's short story, <u>The</u> <u>Stepmother</u>, almost missed his chance to know how wonderful a chosen parent can be.

Let's examine the connecting technique used in this last example. It is, after all, fairly sophisticated. *My cousin* reaches back into the preceding narrative section; *only needed a year* is a summary statement of the story. However, the word *only* implies a short period of time, and the word *however,* as in the first example, implies that a comparison will be made, but that the material it ushers in will be related, but not similar. Also in that example, the words *ten long years* complete the comparison, but show a striking difference. In the second example, we understand there is a comparison being made, and that if we want to know more, we'll have to read further.

As you gain more experience zig-zagging through this introductory approach, you will want to explore the possibility of connecting through *opposites*. Whether you connect from bread to cake or empty to full, never forget that rule from science that says, *opposites attract.*

On approaching the theme sentence through a term implying the opposite.

. . . On the contrary, with my natural parent background, I never gave a thought to stepping until I discovered Margaret Jackson's The Stepmother, and since then I've given little thought to anything else.

On approaching the theme sentence through a connective sentence to position the opposite.

. . . However, my experiences have all been totally opposite those in The Stepmother. Here, author Margaret Jackson weaves a detailed tapestry from the thoughts of a troubled stepson.

Working out your approaches, whether they are direct, oblique, or opposite, takes some patient wording and re-wording. You will find that you can make endless types of single, double, and even triple comparisons between your story and the theme sentence. That's what the craft of writing is all about. You will also discover not to tell any more than the barest hint of the story you will be discussing. Tempt your reader, if you will. That's what a good introductory paragraph is all about.

As you become more experienced with the Zig-Zag you will become more aware of how to use yes, no, or even sentences as connective devices linking one section of the paragraph with another. However, you will also want to increase your source of connective terms. Some new connectives you will want to include are these: also, another, as a result, at last, consequently, for example, for instance, for this purpose, in this case, furthermore, likewise, on the contrary, to the contrary, similarly, directly opposed, on the one hand, and on the other hand.

Besides being particularly useful as an introductory paragraph, the Zig-Zag also makes other valuable contributions to your accumulation of language skills. For one, after gaining expertise with the Zig-Zag you will never again have to worry about being at a loss for a way through a paragraph, a full-length paper, or a test question because you will have correctly learned how to move from one subject to the next, and yet bring it all together at the end. Too, the Zig-Zag prepares you to recognize this unusual construction, and recognize — even in advance — that the topic sentence with its important material is not going to appear until the end. You will recognize this in your reading, and you will become a better reader. You will recognize that this technique is common in advertising, and you will be prepared to evaluate the ad more intelligently.

Many novels and short stories use a Zig-Zag opening: knowing how it's done you will be able to have greater appreciation for the material.

Many test passages use the Zig-Zag: being familiar with the pattern you will be able to read with greater ability than those who are inexperienced with this paragraph plan.

■

4

Paragraph Directions

— Writing is leading the reader —

*R*emember back in *Chapter 2* when you first learned about paragraph plans and you were introduced to the idea of comparing the paragraph with rooms in a house?

Let's go back to that room-paragraph concept to gain a practical understanding of paragraph directions. In some rooms of a house there are two doors or two entrances so that we do not have to go out the same way we came in. This is also true of paragraphs where the closing sentence of one leads out and, most probably, into the opening sentence of the paragraph that follows. This is called the *open-ended* technique. Knowing what it is and how to use it correctly is absolutely essential for multi-paragraph writing of any kind.

However—and let's jump back again to that room-paragraph idea — we can always leave by the same way we came in whether there is only a single door or a variety of exits. The same is also true of paragraphs. In the closing sentence of any paragraph the reader can be brought back to the thoughts of the opening sentence. This technique of returning to the beginning or giving the paragraph a circular quality, is called the *elliptical technique*. Like the open-ended style, the elliptical is equally essential for correct multi-paragraph writing of any kind.

OPEN-ENDED STYLE

Plan

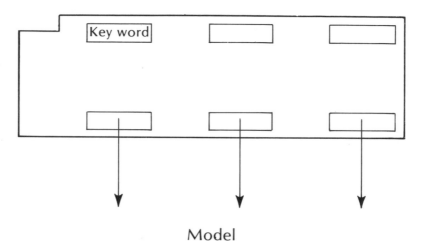

Model

Remember the model for the narrative on page 14, and how it ended with the following:

...the truth was I didn't want to wait eighteen long hours for the next day to begin.

Application

Now, let's see how we might connect this closing of one paragraph with the opening of another:

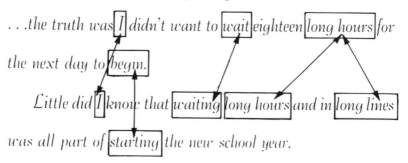

. . .the truth was I didn't want to wait eighteen long hours for the next day to begin.

Little did I know that waiting long hours and in long lines was all part of starting the new school year.

ELLIPTICAL STYLE

Plan

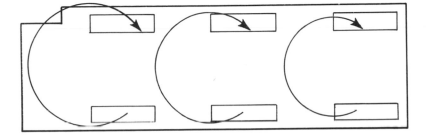

Model

Again, we'll want to return to the model for the narrative, but this time we will need both the opening and the closing sentences.

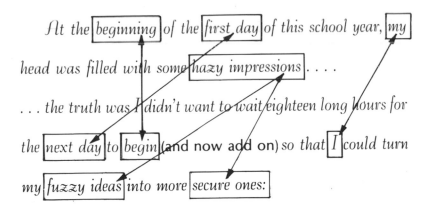

Note carefully how in the above model specific words — and they become key words when put to this connective use — return the closing of the paragraph to its opening.

Now, let's take a further look at how open-ended paragraphs may be converted to the elliptical style. Only the opening and closing sentences of the paragraph examples are included here.

Model
Open-ended Style

Becoming a skilled writer will prove, possibly, to be your greatest personal asset.

..... Finally, to become a skilled writer you are going to have to write, and rewrite, and rewrite.

Model
Elliptical Style

Becoming a skilled *writer will prove, possibly, to be your greatest personal* asset.

..... to write, and rewrite, and rewrite; and then, you and only you, can judge what you have learned and how you might profit *from your* skill.

Or consider this example. You will find the full paragraph on page 46.

Model

Open-ended Style

My little brother is the most delightful character I ever met

. . . . .

. . . . . because the more my little brother seems to change, the more he stays the same.

Model

Elliptical Style

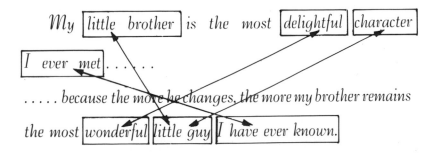

ENTRY DIRECTION

Your ability to control paragraph directions is an important writing skill. However, another important — and equally basic — related skill is the craft of moving in from outside the paragraph and neatly landing on your opening topic sentence. Unlike the Zig-Zag where you could take most of a paragraph to maneuver into your objective, here you will find it useful to make that move with a few well-chosen words. There is something of a trick to this valuable technique, but when you see how it is done, you will be able to effectively use it in your own writing.

Let's assume that the topic of a single paragraph composition is to be fast-foods versus the home-made kind, and that you have chosen to zero in on the hamburger, specifically.

How can you jump into your topic and have the readers in favor of what you're going to say even before you say it?

Try the following formula:

Popular opinion plus your opinion.

Converting that formula to written language you might create the following:

Although many students have been caught up in the fast-food craze, I, like a lot of others I know, am going back to the old-fashioned hamburgers made at home.

Or, you might be writing on some new concept where your readers are naturally resistant because they can't visualize what you're talking about.

Let's take the topic of *sailboarding.*

Your topic sentence is going to be *I like sailboarding.* You also know that you are going to want to use the directed entry into your composition.

Again, use the two-part sentence approach so that you can begin with the readers' favorable attention.

Try the following formula:

Respected known plus your unknown.

Converting this formula to written language you might create the following:

If you think you would like surfing, then you're really going to go for surfboard sailing.

Many of our ideas are shaped by our environments: we tend to adopt the attitudes of those around us. In one part

36

of the country feelings may run strong on conservation; but, in another part of the country where jobs are scarce, the strong feelings may be — not necessarily against conservation — but for industrialization. Or, in your community the overwhelming attitude may be against careers for women, but you want to take the position that there are powerful reasons for women to go into careers.

Whenever you take on a controversial subject you will achieve maximum success if you wisely pre-position your topic.

Try the following formula:

Favored majority point of view plus your sure-to-be unpopular point of view.

Attention all males! Who knows better than you do that there is a woman behind every successful man? However, will those men who are really successsful share their secret which is that behind every successful man is a woman who works.

Any of these well-crafted directed entries require special attention. They are not going to roll from your pen on demand. Play with them. Write and rewrite, and get the words and their subtle implications to do the positioning you want them to do. Readers resist! Part of being a good writer is finding and using the key to their resistance.

DIRECTED CLOSINGS

It is crucial to have your readers on your side by the time you get to your point at the beginning of the paragraph. Of course, once you have them on your side they will be more interested in listening to what you have to say; and, they will more probably be inclined to pass favorably on your details as they read them.

Having brought your readers into the paragraph with control, then brought them through the paragraph with control, you will be risking your good work if you don't end the paragraph with the same careful control.

Use your closing sentence to reinforce the thought. Again, you will find the two-part sentence formula to be the most useful tool for that crucial maneuver which gets your readers out of the composition, but keeps them on your side.

Remember how you jumped from fast-foods to hamburgers? Here is an effective directed closing for such a discussion:

. . . Fast-foods are a sign of progress, but in the case of the all-American hamburger, progress has little to offer what has become synonymous with carefree and comfortble food.

Remember sailboarding? You don't have to lose your reader because of the expense involved. Here is a sympathetic directed closing:

. . . *Admittedly, sailboards are beyond my price range, but if I start saving now, I'll be ready to start sailing by next June.*

—*Writing is also studying what reader-leading techniques professional writers use—*

5

Linking Paragraphs

— Writing is the management of information —

So far we have learned only about writing single paragraphs.

But what about the compositions that you expect to write. Aren't they many paragraphs in length?

Yes! So, let's start off on a fair beginning by talking about the same kind of composition. Although you will hear a lot about creative writing, you might want to keep in the back of your mind that every time you intelligently write a composition, that this is a creative act. Furthermore, it is fair to say that all writing — at whatever level of intelligence — is creative. Now, let's get down to facts: there are two types of writing: *fiction* and *nonfiction*. And, it is the goal of a good education that the student learn to write nonfiction.

Nonfiction, then, in the form of the basic book report — the one type of report that you will be called upon to write more frequently than any other report — will provide the plan of this chapter.

First, this short review: paragraphs move in two directions, open-ended and elliptical.

Second, you will want to briefly recall these paragraphs: the Zig-Zag, the narration and the persuasion.

And, with that you are ready to examine the theoretical plan for linking paragraphs in the basic, elliptical book report.

Plan for Linking Paragraphs

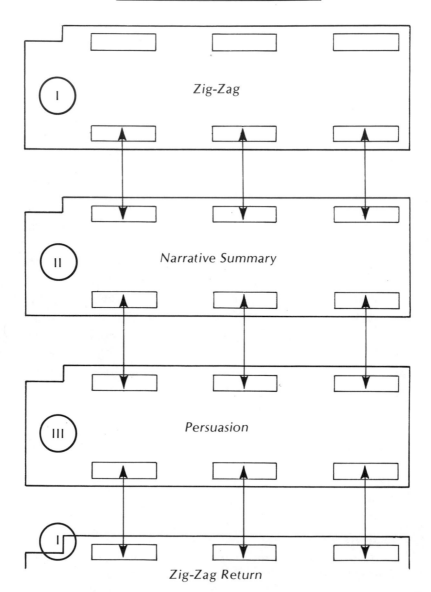

Any realistic examination of linking paragraphs *I, II, III* and the return to *I*, requires that we see the actual connecting words. However, these connectives will have improved meaning if we examine the full paragraphs from which they came.

The following model is the basic book report. It includes the three paragraphs and the return as shown on the plan. Study the model carefully so that you understand the linking of the paragraphs and the elliptical style of this composition.

Model for Linking Paragraphs
in a Basic Book Report

Did you ever dream of hitting the perfect homerun? I know I did! But my homer stayed in the dream-stage up until last summer, and oddly enough, by that time I had nearly quit playing ball. I found myself at the plate, and naturally, I forgot about getting a hit because it was almost too dark to see the ball. I let the first pitch go by. I went after the second one with everything I had. By some coincidence my bat connected with one of those rare, solid smashes that sent a ringing "craaaack," through the dusky air and sent the ball soaring while I leisurely ran the bases to home. However, hitting homers is not easy, especially when you're desperate, and Casey — the desperate batter who needed a homerun in Earnest Thayer's poem, "Casey at the Bat" — had an experience far less rewarding than mine.

In the beginning of the story we found Mudville trailing four to two in the last half of the ninth inning. There were two outs by Cooney and Burrows, and two on base: Flynn on second and Jimmy Blake on third. Next, Casey went to the mound and the crowd went wild, possibly because there was heavy betting that the popular Casey would hit a homerun. Casey, of course, gave them a performance with his clowning gestures and charming grin. Then, he rubbed his hands with dirt, wiped them on his shirt, and . . . let the first pitch go by. The crowd went wild — out of hand — but Casey brought them under control. Next, to everyone's surprise, he let the second pitch go by. The crowd howled, "Fraud"! Finally, there came

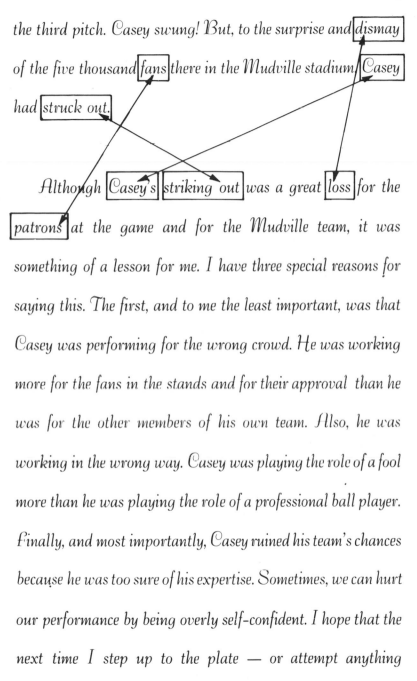

the third pitch. Casey swung! But, to the surprise and dismay of the five thousand fans there in the Mudville stadium, Casey had struck out.

Although Casey's striking out was a great loss for the patrons at the game and for the Mudville team, it was something of a lesson for me. I have three special reasons for saying this. The first, and to me the least important, was that Casey was performing for the wrong crowd. He was working more for the fans in the stands and for their approval than he was for the other members of his own team. Also, he was working in the wrong way. Casey was playing the role of a fool more than he was playing the role of a professional ball player. Finally, and most importantly, Casey ruined his team's chances because he was too sure of his expertise. Sometimes, we can hurt our performance by being overly self-confident. I hope that the next time I step up to the plate — or attempt anything important — that I will concentrate only on doing what I'm there to do. After reading "Casey at the Bat", wouldn't you want to play it safe, too?

Did you ever dream of hitting the perfect homerun?

Basic Paragraphs II

— Writing is to the writer what

the stage is to the actor —

THE CHARACTER SKETCH

*T*here is no plan for the character sketch. There is no special set of connectives. Here, the details roll out in whatever succession the author chooses; however, it is the author's responsibility to so skillfully link the sentences together that each sentence reaches back linking onto the one from which it came.

Anything goes in the character sketch; examples, surprises, quotations, shocks! Keep it about your subject character — usually a fellow human being, but pets make the most ideal studies, surely. And keep your sentences carefully linked together.

Model for a Character Sketch

My little brother is the most delightful character I have ever met. When he first came home, tiny, pink, and sleepy, there was a faint frown about his button-like mouth as his bright blue eyes followed my every move, and his inquiring fingers would reach for mine. He grew, of course, walking, talking, and following me everywhere that I went. Sometimes too far so that I would have to hoist him up onto my shoulders and carry him home. These days though, he is into grownup talk about hamburgers, and new cars, and baseball cards. Sometimes the conversation is beyond both of us. Now that I think of him going into the first grade, feathery blond hair that won't stay in place and always in raggedy sneakers, I can only smile in disbelief. The more my little brother seems to change, the more I think he stays the same.

DESCRIPTION

Descriptive writing creates an image — a kind of word picture — of some object or scene. Now, a new set of connectives are going to prove important — crucial even — because they will detail location and the distance relationships of one detail with another. These connectives are called *place-order connectives.*

There are two kinds of descriptions: graphic and impressionistic. Graphic description tries to be camera like: it is particularly useful for science and social studies. Impressionistic description tries to be more fanciful, freely drawing upon whatever the writer may imagine. Neither one may be said to be more creative nor more challenging than the other.

Whether your description is non-fiction or graphic, of a fictionalized image and impressionistic, you will find it helpful to build your word pictures from some personal observation. Descriptions based on purely imaginary objects and scenes rarely withstand the tests of believability.

Your descriptions tell what you see, feel, hear, taste touch, smell, and what emotions — if any — are involved. Most often your descriptions will be based on what you see. However, if you are going to explore descriptive writing to an advanced degree, you will want to learn to use all your senses and learn how to include similes and metaphors, too.

Descriptive writing is primarily concerned with space. For that reason you will want to familiarize yourself with the technique of linking details within a space or working with what we have already identified as place-order connectives. Some of these are as follows: above, around, across, adjacent to, beyond, behind, below, farther, there, next to, near by, there, to the left, to the right, opposite, in the middle, in the front, in front of, in the rear, at the rear, in back, on the top, on top of, on the bottom, and underneath.

Plan for the Descriptive Paragraph

Topic sentence: tell what you're going to describe.

Inside,

Below,

Above

Model for the Descriptive Paragraph

I think the piano up in Mrs. Hamlin's music room is about the oldest thing I've ever seen. It's case has been scarred with thousands of names and symbols. Some of these are deeply gouged into the wood, but others seem to be only scratched in the finish. Inside, more than a few strings are broken, lying loose in there, and I can hear them rattle when certain chords are played. Below, one leg leans at less-than-upright, while someone's old math book has been jammed under the broken pedal to keep it up off the floor. Above the lock — which you can only see when the keyboard is covered — I can read S-M and J-L-V. I wonder who those two were and if that bright-red outline of a heart around their initials was inked in a long time back, or was it some touch added only yesterday.

EXPOSITION

Exposition, as you might guess from the word itself, means to expose, and that means to explain, to teach, or to reveal. However you come to think of exposition, you will want to pay careful attention to the order in which you arrange your details so that you will have the correct control over what you want to say and so that your reader can have solid control in understanding.

A Plan for an Expository Paragraph

Topic sentence: tell what you're going to explain.

Understandably,

Also,

Finally,

Model for an Expository Paragraph

Becoming a skilled writer will prove, possibly, to be your greatest asset. Understandably, you will write best on those subjects with which you are most familiar, such as yourself or topics from your reading. Also, you will want to make a careful distinction between fiction and nonfiction: most of the writing you will do in high school, college, and your business career, will be reports. Reports are strictly nonfiction, so learning to say what you mean and mean what you say is all-important. Finally, to become a skilled writer you are going to write, and rewrite, and rewrite. Only you will know how far you've come and how much you've worked. Your critics will know only that you seem to be far more skilled than your peers.

The connectives that help make your control more effective in exposition are among the following: also, another, as a result, at last, consequently, finally, first, for example, for instance, for this purpose, furthermore, likewise, next, on the contrary, on the one hand, and on the other hand.   ■

7

Split Paragraphs

THE COMPARISON

*F*requently, you will find it useful to compare two topics. Of course, you cannot write on two topics at the same moment any more than you can speak two words at the same time. What you can do is use the simple and practical device for paragraphing this common writing problem. You have only to decide whether you are going to make a case for *similarities* — which will take you to the comparison — or *differences* — which will mean a contrast. Now, to compare.

Plan for a Paragraph to Compare

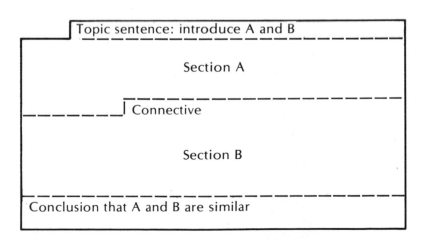

Topic sentence: introduce A and B

Section A

Connective

Section B

Conclusion that A and B are similar

Model for a Paragraph to Compare

My friends John and Debbie seem to be not only long-time good friends, but very good for each other. John is into his hobby. He spends hours cutting wood into thin strips, fastening the strips together, and assembling every conceivable type of kite. Debbie, who is inseparable from John, is also into a hobbie. In this case it's roller-skating. Debbie constantly practices steps, turns, stops, cross-overs and dance rhythms. For whatever their differences, I find them so much alike because they are both active, both into highly skilled hobbies, both loyal to each other, and both wonderfully good friends.to me.

THE CONTRAST

Now, let's take the same material we used for the comparison, change our emphasis to *differences,* and we will have a formula for a contrast.

You will want to become thoroughly expert with comparing and contrasting because it is the only intelligent way to handle *the* most frequent type of essay test question. Whether you are asked to discuss two characters within a story, two cities, or two amoebas, you will need a good pattern if you are going to make quick and sound sense out of what might otherwise become a tangled mess.

Plan for a Paragraph to Contrast

Topic sentence: introduce A and B

Section A

Connective

Section B

Conclusion that A and B are different

Model for a Paragraph to Contrast

Although John and Debbie are both good friends of mine, I'm beginning to wonder if they are good for each other. On the one hand, John is so into kites that he can think of nothing else. He seems to spend all his time cutting wood into thin strips, fastening the strips together and assembling every imaginable type of kite. On the other hand, Debbie seems to think only of skating. She is constantly practicing her roller steps, doing turns, cross-overs, and dance rhythms. Even though they spend most of their time together, and they seem perfectly happy to do so, I'm beginning to wonder if they have anything in common. Certainly John and Debbie make a strong case for the old saying that opposites attract.

TO COMPARE AND CONTRAST

There will be times when you face the problem of how to compare and contrast within a single paragraph. This problem will naturally occur because every comparison implies some contrast, and every contrast implies some comparison. However, you are going to find yourself in real trouble trying to deal with a hodgepodge of information unless you have a good plan.

Plan for
A Paragraph to Compare and to Contrast

Topic sentence: introduce A and B

Section for similarities

Connective

Characteristics of A

Connective

Characteristics of B

Conclusion

Plan for
a Paragraph to Compare and to Contrast

John and Debbie are two of my closest friends. On the one hand, they share many traits. They are both into activities and hobbies which require great concentration and skill. They are both good natured. They are both loyal to me and to each other. On the other hand, they are also very different from each other. John is quiet, brainy, and always thinking of designs and materials for better kites. Debbie, who has become a roller-dance person, is very physical. She seems to want only to skate, to talk about skating techniques, equipment she hopes to buy, and skating clothes. Of course, I recognize that these two have been best friends for years, but when I think of how little they have in common, I wonder what keeps them together and how long it will last.

CONTRASTING POINT-BY-POINT

There are very few *don't do's* in this book. *Don't* is not a recommended word for anyone who wants to take up the practice of writing. However, don't expect to dash off a paragraph to contrast point-by-point with a quick and continuous and effortless roll of the pen. Shaping this paragraph is a careful combination of hard thinking and rethinking, writing and rewriting.

This suggested plan for the paragraph to contrast point-by-point is — like all the plans in this book — only an approximation of how the paragraph might be shaped.

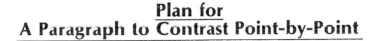

Plan for
A Paragraph to Contrast Point-by-Point

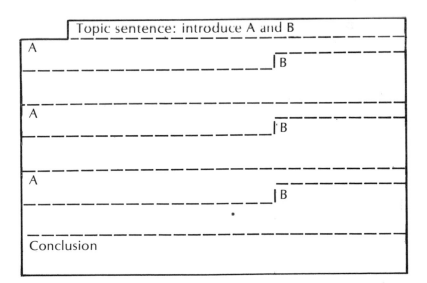

Model for
A Paragraph to Contrast Point-by-Point

The differences between John and Debbie are clearly shown in their choice of hobbies. John likes kites. Debbie likes skates. John likes to work with his hands. Debbie prefers her feet. John likes to design shapes that fly. Debbie wants only to be a flying shape. John seeks originality. Debbie seeks to imitate the movements of others. John likes to sit and think out plans for his future super-kite. Debbie never sits: she is constantly gyrating this way and that. Now, John says he's going to get a skateboard. Debbie is talking about using a kite for a sail while she is on skates. For all their difference, anyone can see why John and Debbie remain good and loyal friends.

Although all the paragraphs in this book may be found hard at work wherever you find writing working — particularly for money — the paragraph to contrast point-by-point works the hardest. Contrasting point-by-point is particularly useful in the field of advertising because it makes a swift comparison of two subjects in a matter of seconds. Moreover, its mind-teasing rhythms and memory-pleasing play on words make it an admirable paragraph plan.

Contrasting point-by-point usually puts in over-time when it comes to political campaigns. The following example was radio-broadcast in and around New York City during a recent race for the U. S. Senate.

John Haskins and Thomas Preston both want your vote so that they can represent you in the United States Senate. Consider their past performance in the New Jersey State Assembly. Haskins served eighteen years. Preston six. Haskins was absent twice during that time. Preston missed the rollcall one hundred and twenty-eight sessions. Haskins voted to increase programs for the aged. Preston said, "No". Haskins voted for gun controls. Preston abstained. Haskins sought improved conservation for New Jersey's wetlands.

Preston sought to increase their commercialization. Haskins wanted tax exemptions for home energy-saving measures, but Preston didn't even vote on this because he was on a junket to Mexico asking for more oil so that those energy-saving measures wouldn't be necessary. Isn't it time you made your vote work for you by voting for the candidate's performance?

Contrasting point-by-point is also the most difficult paragraph to write. *To write* hardly explains the act, for the paragraph to contrast point-by-point is carefully shaped so that facts, syllables and sentences may be positioned to gain maximum effect. Let your paragraph become an artistic achievement; and, if you are going to succeed with that you are going to want to craft your contrast so that it entertains your readers.

The plan of contrasting point-by-point is not new: in 1859, the English author Charles Dickens opened his novel, *A Tale of Two Cities,* with just such a paragraph.

Dicken wrote,

"It was the best of times; it was the worst of times . . . "

Today's student may find the language heavy and meaningless, but for that student who can see the clear plan of this opening, Dicken's poetic and structural skills shout from the first page.

A PARAGRAPH TO SHOW CAUSE AND EFFECT

The Plan

Topic sentence:introduce the cause of the problem

Description of the problem

Connective

Description of the effect

A Model
for a Paragraph of Cause and Effect

Less than two years ago California agricultural experts discovered the first evidence of Mediterranean fruit fly maggots in San Francisco area's fruit. The maggots — or more correctly, the larvae — hatch from eggs laid just beneath the fruit skin. As the crop matures, these maggots devour the fruit flesh until, ruined, it falls from the tree. However devastating this stage, its effect has proven even worse. In California's case. it has resulted in insecticide spraying — in six doses yet — of the one hundred and fifty square-mile Bay Peninsula, bringing widespread panic and damaging the credibility of the state's govenment. Too, the Med fly has seriously threatened

California's $14 billion agricultural industry. But, worse yet: with the massive search-and-destroy efforts being brought against this super-destructive insect, there is no way for healthy fruit to be kept safe. However, it is the unknown that hangs like a grim cloud on the future, for the scientists claim there is no way to know for certain — for California has no previous Mediterranean fruit fly experience — what effects the Med fly will wreck on future crops.

The paragraph for cause and effect uses a very simple organizational layout, However, the thinking needed to shape its content must, at all times, be carefully controlled. Most often you will be working from an event. Always separate those details which are cause and those which are effect. You will notice that this paragraph requires factual details. If you use this plan for your thought pattern you will always be able to turn out an admirable piece of writing.

A PARAGRAPH FOR A PROBLEM AND SOLUTION

Now, let's recycle the Med fly material so that we may concentrate on the problem in the first half of the paragraph, and then concentrate on the solution for the second half.

Plan for
A Paragraph for a Problem and Solution

Topic sentence: introduce the problem

- -

Description of the problem

- - - - - - - - - - - - - Connective - - -

Description of the solution

Model for
A Paragraph for a Problem and Solution

Less than two years ago California agricultural experts discovered evidence of the Mediterranean fruit fly in the San Francisco Bay area's produce. The Med fly's life cycle could prove devestating to California's $14 billion agricultural industry because the insect is capable of single-handedly destroying a fruit and vegetable crop, and...then moving on to do the same damage in a neighboring region. However, acting on the dreaded problem, California officials sprayed the entire suspect Bay Peninsula with the insecticide malathion. The spraying procedure was scheduled for a six-dose application. To further check the Med fly's infestation, all fruit was stripped from the three-county area's bushes and trees, bagged, and then buried in the ground. Also, blocks were set up at all air, truck, and rail check-points to find and confiscate fruit and vegetables scheduled to leave the one hundred and fifty square-mile area. The outcome of these corrective steps will not be fully known until officials have made an assessment on the Mediterranean fruit fly's infestation on future California crops.

The paragraph for a problem and solution uses the same plan as the paragraph showing cause and effect. The difference betwen the two is in the thinking: the effect section of the cause and effect paragraph treats the material from the point of view that it is all a continuation of the initial problem.

PARALLEL DEVELOPMENT

Let us shift our thinking to yet another type of split-topic paragraph. However, in this case there is to be no open comparison nor contrast, no cause or effect relationship; no problem or solution. The paragraph for *parallel development* simply describes two subjects found in the topic sentence: for example, big houses are expensive to heat and to maintain. Such a paragraph would give the first half of its discussion to problems of heat and the second half to the problems of maintenance.

Plan for
Parallel Development

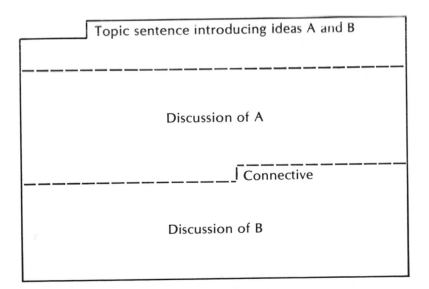

Topic sentence introducing ideas A and B

Discussion of A

Connective

Discussion of B

A Model for Parallel Development

Being part of a large family can be both pleasurable and frustrating. It is always enjoyable to have someone around so that you don't get lonely. There is always someone for you to talk to when you need to. Coming from a large family myself, I've noticed that my parents divide up our chores equally. I certainly get help with my homework if I don't understand it, and when I get sick, I get loads of loving attention. However, having a large family isn't all fun and games. It sure is frustrating waiting on line in the morning just to get into the bathroom! Someone is always on the phone no matter what hour of the day. I hardly ever receive new clothes; always hand-

me-downs. *My mother's motto is "share your things," but it is difficult when you have to share a bedroom, share books, share clothes, share dressers, share desks, and then share your friends. For once in my life I want to watch television programs that I want to watch. A large family certainly proves to be enjoyable and loads of annoyance, too.*

BEFORE AND AFTER

Perhaps it is fitting that our study of paragraphing end as it began: but, now we'll take the narrative and put it to practical, and double-duty use as a paragraph capable of tracing the development of any subject. However, the *before and after* paragraph has a special application for any English course because "trace the development of . . ." is one of the English teachers' most often asked test questions. Using this technique will allow your personal knowledge to shine through to its best advantage.

Plan for
A Before and After Paragraph

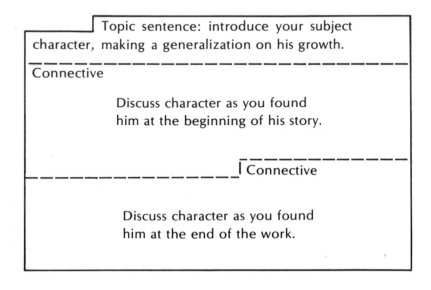

Topic sentence: introduce your subject character, making a generalization on his growth.

Connective

Discuss character as you found him at the beginning of his story.

Connective

Discuss character as you found him at the end of the work.

Model for
A Before and After Paragraph

The point, I think, of S. E. Hinton's novel, That Was Then, This is Now, is to show how Bryan had matured. At the beginning of the story we saw him as a tough street kid, complete with his jeans and T-shirt uniform, and a language style concentrating on booze, girls, and gang fights. There was also his perpetual street-corner pose and the endless cigarette. Beyond these superficials we also saw that Bryan had no commitment to either his home or his education, nor did he have the desire to make one. Then, within the natural development of his interests, M and M's tragedy causes Bryan to begin a rapid change. Bryan gives up his street friends and goes to work. He gives up his old attitudes and begins to see the problems of others, particularly his employer. He begins to understand the meaning of home as he saw what M and M had. Too, he begins to put time in to his school work. However, in this case I don't find the story convincing because Bryan's grades jump from all-around failure to straight A's. Curiously, it was back at the beginning, or the That Was Then part that Bryan was so sure that he knew all the answers, and, it's with the *This is Now*, or the end, that Bryan learns that he not only doesn't know the answers, but that he has no idea about the questions. In Bryan's case, maturity means learning to cope with breaking away from old friends and learning how to find his own way.

A word on closing sentences for these split subject paragraphs:

A discussion of the second subject, let's call it Topic B for convenience, is all that is needed according to the opening sentence of each of these split paragraphs. However, you may add on concluding sentences:

Plan Detail for Conclusions

Discussion of Topic B

Conclusion

This concluding section may take a number of different directions: one, this added conclusion may generalize on the Topic B discussion; two, it may knit together a generalization on both Topic B and A; three, it may return to the opening sentence creating an elliptical paragraph; or four, it may be designed as an open-ended paragraph, where the language feeds into the opening of material that is to follow. ∎

You now have considerable paragraph writing experience and expertise because you have studied a comprehensive writing system: each of the paragraph plans presented in *Part I* of this book provided a specific plan; and each of the paragraph models presented in *Part I* of this book provided an example of how a model might be created for that plan.

In your future writing projects you will put your experience and expertise to its best purpose if you always ask yourself, "What exactly do I want this paragraph to say?" Once you have honestly answered that question, you will be able to select that paragraph plan which best suits your needs . . . and, proceed. You will be putting your time to good and careful use because you have decided in advance on the purpose and direction the paragraph must take and you can predict what type of a closing you will need to carry out your objective.

Knowing the purpose, direction, and conclusion of the paragraph puts you in control. Then, once you are in control you are free — for the first time — to make choices, to try new strategies, to make changes, to dare to experiment, and finally, to create.

One may argue forever on whether writing is a craft or an art. Such a discussion has nothing to do with the individual's creative process. However, there is no argument for good writing being the result of no experience; good writing is the result of practice. ∎

now . . .

II

WRITE YOUR WAY TO SUCCESS

Mathematics works on an order of operations: add, subtract, multiply, and divide.

Good writing also works on an order of operations know as priorities.

Know what it is you want to say.

Know the limitations, or the time and space within which it must be said.

Know your plan.

Know your objective. This objective may be entirely separate from your subject material, for it is your personal objective. You may want to be dramatic, or to be understated. You may want to be political, to be entertaining, to be sarcastic, or to be outrageous. You may want to manipulate your reader. You may want to win a contest or simply get an A grade. Or, you may want to be the best writer in your class.

Material, limitations, plan, and objective will become your order of priorities. ∎

8

Dialogue

— Writing reflects the spoken language —

Why Dialogue

 $\mathcal{C}$ an you remember an experience in your life where, now that you look back on it, you felt very happy?

Or, can you remember an experience in your life where you felt very sad? Even thinking about it now, you could almost cry?

And, can you remember an experience where you felt embarrassed, so much so that today you feel a rush of heat to your face and arms?

If you are like most people, the fine experiences, the sad ones, and those incredibly embarrassing ones did not take place in a vacuum; rather, they were the result of your interaction — your conversation — with others.

Yet, how often in the past when you wrote about these events so important to you, did you write out block paragraphs of narrative without so much as a hint about the meaningful conversation that took place?

Often, it is not the narration, but it is the conversation upon which some memorable event can be recreated.

Adding Dialogue to Your Narrative

And, if you are like most students who want to learn how to write, you'll want to become an expert at dialogue, how to use it according to the rules of punctuation, and how to make it work for you.

Dialogue is converstion.

Listen to what these two students said to each other:

It's mine.

I didn't mean to.

If, however, you wrote this simple, two-line conversation in a composition, you would not have enough material to make it clear to the reader what actually went on between the two speakers. On the other hand, you — having heard the words and witnessed the action—know all about what scene you want to recreate. You know the whole meaningful story behind these unidentified voices. By adding who, where, and how to your dialogue, you can bring these two meaningless lines to life.

Here's how.

"It's mine!" cried Ann, as she snatched her homework paper off of the desk behind hers.

Tom hissed, "Gee, I'm sorry," and turned his eyes down so that she wouldn't see how guilty he felt.

How to Write Dialogue

In your short stories—and, in some case, reports — you will want to use dialogue because dialogue is one of the *living* qualities of experience. Also, dialogue will make your characters seem more life-like; first, because you have given them the power of speech; and secondly, because it is only in their speech that you can approximate the irregularities — the incomplete sentences, the non-words, sounds, the words run together, and the imperfections — of human speech. Finally, dialogue quickens the reading pace — almost pulling the reader along — and it reduces the worded space giving relief to the monotony of the solid, block paragraphs. Keep in mind, however, the order of priorities for writing.

In writing dialogue you will want to follow two simple rules: every time you change speakers, you begin on a new and indented line. And, rule two: when you write dialogue, open your literature book to a story with dialogue, and — for the sake of punctuation — use it as your model.

Dialogue as Narrative

"That science test wasn't what I expected," Sheila groaned as we neared our lockers. "Angela call you?"

"Nope," I said with a shrug, trying to dodge the question. I knew what she meant. "But she called last week. Thursday. We talked about nothing much. Clothes and friends. Nothing else . . "

"It's mean," Sheila, who was ordinarily very friendly, said cutting me off quickly. "Keeping me on the string. And it's almost Friday." She fiddled with the combination. "I hope I get some great offer." Sheila slammed her books onto the top shelf. "Like pizza for two on one paper plate. No dishes to do and no one to share it with!"

I fought all my instincts to hold back on what I wanted to say. I could have said "Stop!" Or maybe, "Wait, you don't understand!" Or I could have smiled a little. Anything to take the pressure off.

"I can't believe Angela would do a thing like this to me,"

she kind of mouthed her words through clenched teeth as she took her frustrations out on the lock, and then gave it a final yank to know that it held. *"Sometimes you don't know who your friends really are."*

"Don't tell me anything. Especially if it isn't the truth. Look, I'm not ashamed to admit that I know there's going to be a party, and it's being given by the one person I thought was my closest friend." She stormed two steps toward her next class only to stop short and shout. *"And I have not. Repeat N-O-T been invited! Could I make it any plainer than that? What am I supposed to think?"*

"I can't say a word." What else could I tell her under the

conditions? But I knew if I stayed there another second I'd break down, confess, and it would be all over.

"Yeccccht!" Sheila sounded off and went on to English.

The hall traffic had thinned out, so I ran, took the stairs two at a time. It would have been so easy to admit the truth. Sure, there was going to be a party. A surprise party. For Sheila! But I would have spoiled it for her if I had given her the slightest hint about what was going on.

Writing with Dialect

Every language has its dialects.

Americans may not know that Frenchmen from Marseilles roll their *R*'s, whereas, those from Paris do not. Or that cockneys drop their *H's*, whereas other Londoners may not. However, most Americans do recognize that natives of New England have something special about the way that they say "car," or "park." There is also something special about the pronunciation habits of natives from the country around Chesapeake Bay. Moreover, natives of the South also have pronunciation specialties. These regional qualities of speech are called *dialects*.

For the writer, dialects are a lot of fun! Dialects are challenging to write and interesting to read. They can help the writer with dialogue because they add variety to the spelling and converstion; they add unwritten characterization to the speaker; and dialect is convenient: it allows the author to change speakers without having to include, "So-and-so said . . "

Dialect in Dialogue

"Now, I want you'all to come on down to the chuck wagon.

Ya heah?" Rod asked the face in the morror. He had spent all of his fifteen years in Boston and he had never before traveled far from home. Now that his family planned a vacation at the Bar-J Ranch somewhere near Steamboat Springs, high in the Colorado Rockies, he was determined to acquire some Western traits.

"You'all . . . y'all . . ." He carefully annunciated the sounds, trying for different effects, and trying to appear natural. Rodney did not want to be spotted as simply a vacationer.

"Whatta y'all do?" he quietly asked the driver as their jeep bounced along the dusty road.

"I'm in charge of horses." And that was all the fellow said since they left Denver an hour back.

"Y'all done a lotta ridin' through these here mountains afore?" he kept on, anxious to get some authentic feed-back.

The driver, concentrating on the traffic at the cross-road, only nodded.

"I s'poz you git a whole lotta folks from back East comin' out here?"

Rodney worked hard at refining his language, and he was thoroughly pleased when, on the second day of his vacation, a plump, elderly woman, also from around Boston, confided to him that she especially liked what she called real Western boys because of their charmig ways, particularly, their speech. She went on and on about Western drawl and its easygoing sound.

"Yes, M'am," Rodney answered, keeping an eye on his family who was having breakfast on the far side of the room. "Yeeees, M'am." He took a long pause. "Y'all pass the sweet milk, please." He grinned. He was proud. Sweet milk had been more than he had wanted to say at this time. The victory was harldy worth playing trump cards. Still, it was a victory.

Later on, that same morning, he went to the corral to be assigned his horse and guide. As it turned out, the man in charge of signing up horses and riders was non other than the driver of the jeep who brought Rodney and his family in from Denver.

Y'all done much ridin' afore?" He moved in and out among the patient animals, going directly to a small roan mare that he had in mind for Rodney.

"Yep," Rodney answered, a little unsure of what was going on.

"Round here?" the man asked sternly as he brought up the horse.

"Nope," Rod grunted, fitting his foot into the stirrup. "Never 'round these here parts."

"Well, I don't suppose I have to tell someone with your experience to stay close to your guide."

"Nope . . .

"And stay away from loose rocks. And, look . . ." He stopped suddenly and shrugged. "Look, I'll level with you. You can get on from where you are standing. Hmmmm . . . ph," he cleared his throat. "But, generally, and I mean even the folks from back East, find it a lot easier to get on a horse from this side."

Writing with Accent

Many Americans came here from another country where English was not the spoken language. They've learned English, but their speech is shaded, or somehow touched, by their native or original language. This overlapping of one language on another is called *accent*.

For the writer, accents provide additional tools. They can help make dialogue more effective. Naturally, it takes some thinking to spell out the special pronunciation, but it enriches dialogue in much the same way as working with dialect did.

Remember that accent makes an important statement for the character in the dialogue: it tacitly says that the character has learned two languages, not just one.

Accent in Dialogue

"You yoost vait 'til I find my san'vish," Hap *said in the lunchroom.* Happy *was the resident comic for our table.* His

specialty was imitating film stars, but on this day he had us

holding our sides with his imitation of Swensen, the new lab

assistant. Then, from the cafeteria to his paper route — and I'm

not sure how he talked me into making that leap — I came to see

the meaning of accent in a different light.

It was already dark by the time we got to 71st Street.

"Hi, Mr. Scotto. Okay if I make the rounds?"

I waited near the door while Hap went in among the diners,

quietly offering his papers. We were about to leave when Mr.

Scotto reappeared. He always spoke softly. "How many

papers you sella this night?"

Hap ran his experienced finger down the two stacks.

"Twenty-two, maybe twenty of the News. Times, I'm not sure."

"Thatsa no good, huh! You're a smarta kid. You tella me

this thing. How come you canna talk like me, but I canna no

talk like you?"

Hap just stood there with his mouth gaping. The silence

seemed long and awkward.

"You nica guy."

Hap and I traded glances that asked what was coming next.

"You gotta some other kinda pants?" Scotto frowned at Hap's cut-off jeans. "Gotta nica shirt, white, maybe?"

"Sure, Mr. Scotto."

"I needa busa-boy. You changa you clothes. You worka when I want. If thatsa good, then you gotta the job." The restaurateur held out his well-manacured hand.

Once outside Happy kept saying, "You believe that? You believe that . . . you beli . . ."

"Yep. I believe . . ." Then I waited for him while he chucked his papers into a open trash can. "I believe I've never seen you put on a better performance than the one you put on tonight."

9

The Anecdote

— Writing is entertaining —

Of all the opportunities for writing limited pieces, the anecdote offers the least rigid, the most creative scope.

The anecdote is a short, funny story. Although you weren't introduced to the term anecdote, you met the style in Chapter 8, *Dialogue: Dialogue as Narrative,* page 84; *Writing with Dialect,* page 87; and *Writing with Accent,* page 92, which are all representative of the anecdotal style.

However, in learning to craft an anecdote, it is wisest to begin with a 150-word composition. You will have no difficulty in fitting all of your details into this tightly knitted space; moreover, your punch line will have a powerful effect because it happens before your reader has the chance to put you paper down.

But, don't be fooled by the humor of the anecdote because it is really a highly serious and practical piece of writing.

Teachers like to give the anecdote as a composition assignment because it is superbly efficient: in exactly one page the student will demonstrate control of narrative, description, dialogue, and the mechanicals — sentence structure, spelling, and punctuation — and all within the super-tight organization of one side of a sheet of paper. The teacher can then assess your skills with little more than a glance; the teacher can also get a good profile of the class without wading through reams of paper. It is assumed, by teachers and students alike, that the student will have fun writing the anecdote.

How can anyone have a good time knocking their brains out trying to do a good piece of work when they don't know what it is they are trying to do?

The anecdote has another practical application: it's a money-maker. Newspapers and magazines have numerous spaces for what is known as the *short-short*. And, they'll pay you for yours. The best place to start if you want to get ready for that professional step, is by sending anecdotes to your community or school newspaper.

There is, however, quite a trick to writing anecdotes. Learn how, and you'll be able to turn out beautifully crafted pieces.

But, let's first read the *Model for an Anecdote*. Maybe you can figure out how it works so that you can match your explanation with the one on page 98.

Model for an Anecdote

On their way home after a hard day of hunting lions and leopards, two cavemen paused on a high bluff for some rest.

The brawnier, wincing as he hiked up the strap on his bear-skin suit, said, "I'm not experienced with the art world, but I'd venture to say that the magnificent view down there will one day make a fine oil painting."

"I hadn't thought about it," grunted his runty partner as he jabbed at a still-leaping lizard in his game bag. Then he squinted at the spectacularly flat landscape below. "I dunno much about art, but I think — and not too many years down the road — that space is going to make a darn profitable parking lot."

Like gathering piping hot pancakes, butter, and maple syrup for a fun-feed, you'll need to bring together three equally simple ingredients for your anecdote.

The ingredients, or your materials, are the following: one, a picture; two, a short, very simple narrative which you have built up from that picture; and three, a punch-line.

And where would you expect to find these basic materials that exactly match your needs?

A cartoon!

A simple, crudely drawn cartoon not a beautiful colored picture. Not a comic strip. Just that cartoon. There is your picture. You can come up with any number of suitable narrations built from that one scene. As for your punch-line, there it is — already thought up by someone else — in the caption below.

Whatever humor is to be enjoyed from your anecdote, it is mostly controlled through timing. Let your punch-line carry the freight, pulling the piece along, pulling it together at the end, and then pulling it into the realm of the ridiculous. That's why it's crucial for your punch-line to be the last line you write.

Those are the basics. Here are some variables that this author used: the addition of irrelevant details; unlikely characterizations; unlikely language; and the unlikely — the ridiculous — mix of Stone Age characters with urban ideas. ∎

10

Short Reports

— Writing is reporting —

*I*n your academic life, your personal life, and in your future business life, the short report will probably win the report-most-likely-to-be-written-the-most-often award! You will want to use the short report for homework assignments and for extra-credit assignments. You will find it useful for the business letters you are writing even now, but you will find it absolutely necessary for the business letters which you will write as an adult. You will find the short report useful when you speak in class, and you will find it indispensable for formal speaking occasions outside of school.

However, if the short report were easy to do well, everyone would be doing it well. The short report does have its problems, but it's easy to write once you know how. You will always be working within limitations. You will always be working with too little material, but without the opportunity to expand or to extend it. You will also be working with material that doesn't divide itself into neat paragraphs. You will also — by definition of the short report — be working within limited space; say, a page and a half. And, you will be working within a limited time frame; say, one class period for writing; or, two minutes for a speech.

Afterall, where is it written that your reader or your listener should have to sit through a 500 page epic to gain an overview of a single topic?

Then, the short report — and this is especially valuable for any student to know — is particularly useful to teachers: it is a useful assignment for assessing students' writing skills. Here, especially with the equalizing factor of all the students writing on the same subject material, using the same set of facts, teachers can quickly measure writing skills in presentation, organization, and cohesive construction; in sentence structure, grammer and usage, spelling and capitalization, and punctuation; and in respect for the assignment. In short, the short report — and no play on words is intended here — has become *the test* for writing competency.

This is what you must do if you are going to write a superb, short report: follow the rules, use the assignment, and use the facts.

The Rules

These are the rules: you may use only the facts given; and, you are to write about 200 words — which is about a page and a half of moderate size script — and firmly adhere to the assignment throughout your report.

The Assignment

This is the assignment: you have been asked to assume that you are to interview a Mr. Peter Miller, the new social studies teacher, who recently spent a vacation in Dublin.

The Facts

Dublin — wet, cold, foggy
    Umberellas everywhere
    Situated on the Liffey River
    Winding streets — charming neighborhoods
    World-famous theaters.
    Harp players on street corners
    Group singing in public houses
    Famous for Irish football
    Only place in the world where one
        can hear Gaelic
    Fashion industry
    Shops selling knits and tweeds
    Excellent restaurants — liked the
        French one best
    Said he enjoyed everything

For best results, the short report should be done in three steps: organization, the rough draft, and the final writing.

Organizing this or any other short report is a little like arranging cards in your hand. You will want to put all the hearts into one section, all the diamonds together in another, all the clubs into their group, an so on. But, instead of working with card suits, let's work with these ideas: *weather, sightseeing,* and *entertainment.* You will always find abstract subheadings the most practical means for grouping what might otherwise be diverse facts within the short report.

Write the three words, weather, sightseeing, and entertainment, as though they might head up three columns on scratch paper. Then, number your facts from 1 to 13. Next, put the appropriate number under the appropriate heading. Use every fact. These three groups, now, are going to become the basis for your short report.

And now to borrow from some of your newly learned writing skills. You'll need a Zig-Zag type of paragraph for your introduction. You'll want to borrow from *Dialogue* to strengthen your slender facts and improve the linking of one paragraph to the next. Finally, you will need a good closing technique: this you may borrow from the closing of the *Basic Book Report,* page 44, making your short report elliptical.

Model for a Short Report

Mr. Peter Miller, the new social studies teacher, has recently returned from Dublin. He gave me this information about the Irish capitol in an interview. "If you're planning a trip to Dublin, be sure to carry an umbrella. Everyone does. You have to because Dublin is always wet. It's cold and foggy, too."

However, the weather isn't going to stop you from having a good time. Mr. Miller told me that Dublin has a lot of interesting things to see. You'll want to visit the River Liffey which flows through the city. You'll want to walk down the winding streets through the charming neighborhoods. Moreover, since Ireland has become a part of the international fashion industry, you won't want to miss visiting the little shops where you will surely find some good buys in knits and tweeds.

Mr. Miller said that entertainment could be found almost everywhere. There are musicians playing harps out on the street corners. You can join in a group-sing at the public houses. For the sports enthusiast there is the Irish football match, and for the theater-goer, there is always the world-famous Irish theater. Finally, for anyone who delights in hearing rare languages, this is almost the only place in the world where you can hear Gaelic spoken.

I asked Mr. Miller what he liked best of all. He said, "The restaurants. Dublin is full of excellent restaurants. I liked a French one best of all." Then Mr. Miller added, "I enjoyed everything."

— Writing is strict adherence to the facts —

— Writing is telling the truth —

NEWS REPORTING

News writing, like all good writing, springs from good design.

The design conveniently breaks into two parts or two paragraphs: one, the formula sentence, or the 4W sentence; and the second paragraph, the Y or H.

Sound mysterious? It doesn't need to be. News reporting moves in a step-by-step process. Here's what the two parts might look like.

Plan for a News Report

4W's: where, when, who, and what

Y or H: why and how

But, what do we mean by *4W*, or the where, when, who, and what paragraph?

You learned to write a formula sentence when you learned to write the theme sentence for the *Zig-Zag* on page 21. Now, in the news writing, you are going to learn to write another type of formula sentence, namely, the 4W.

Let's work backwards. News reporting requires a story, and that story says that an event took place. *Something* had to have happened: which brings us to *what*. The event had to involve either a group or an individual: which brings us to *who.*The event had to happen at a given time or within a given time-frame: which brings us to *when*. And because this event did take place, it had to occur within a space or place: which brings us to *where*.

If you open your news reports with this formula, you will have fulfilled the opening requirements of news reporting.

Then too, what do we mean by Y or W?

This part is both simpler and more difficult than the 4W formula. To tell why something happened or what happened opens the writer to many variables, all of which are dependent upon the author's perception.

Let's go in this direction:

The study of news reporting is too broad and too complex to be undertaken here in its entirety. However, the style of the news report has a valuable contribution to make to all short reports. It is compact; it includes few non-essential words or statements: but, it must include all the essentials of the event. Moreover, the news report style is prized for its special organization. That 4W sentence formula provides the reader with the most important facts. The *why* or *what* part that follows fills in with the details. In placing the facts first, the reader can take them all in at a quick glance, and then decide on whether or not to continue with the article.

News reporting is a study in efficiency. The reader gets the facts up front without having to sort them out by reading through the entire report.

News, by nature, is usally catastrophic! You have only to study the front-page articles of your newspaper to see that.

So, let's see what might be done with a lighter story of a car going off the road. And, this is a story you could find on any page of any newspaper.

Model for a News Report

Greenwich, Connecticut, July 21: Connecticut State Police reported that an automobile driven by Arthur Anderson allegedly went out of control at the intersection of North Street and East Middle Patent Road where it plunged into Deep Water Reservoir and sank.

Mr. Anderson, a resident of Hartford, told reporters that he was driving toward Greenwich at the time of the accident. He said, "There was no indication of mechanical trouble. I keep this car in the best, absolute showroom condition."

The vehicle, a 1927 Rolls Royce Silver Wraith, failed to respond to a right turn, Anderson added. He said that the Rolls proceeded due south, veered to the left, ran along the shoulder of the road for about a hundred yards, and then into the water. The car apparently floated for a few minutes, and then sank from sight.

Anderson, who identified himself as 58 years-of-age and a strong swimmer, estimated that the Rolls is resting on a firm, sandy bottom in about 15 feet of water and about 15 feet from the shore. He further reported that he had no trouble rolling down a window to get out of the car, and that he was unhurt.

Connecticut State Police are standing by until a crane can be brought in to raise the automobile to the surface.

For our purposes in this book, we are not concerned with the components of the news report except those two sections that introduce and detail the event. Our purpose for studying news reporting here is to apply the technique to reporting requirements in general. Although news reporting requires more thought and writing exactness than the summary narrative, that exactness is the best all-around summary device for nonfiction in English, and for science, and for social studies.

However, news reporting teaches yet another valuable skill: the craft of quoting. There are two ways in which to make a quotation correctly.

Direct quotations: to use the direct quotation the writer takes the actual — the exact — words of the speaker, and, without making a change, inserts them between quotation marks: for example; Mr. Anderson said, "I keep this car in the best, absolute showroom condition."

Indirect quotations: the indirect quotation is less demanding. Here, the writer does not follow the speaker word-for-word, and for that reason, the quotation marks are dropped. However, this freedom requires the use of the word *that.* For example; Mr. Anderson said *that* the car was kept in the top-notch condition.

— Writing is promoting —

SPORTS WRITING

Sports reporting is similar to news reporting only in that they happen to be printed in the same newspaper. It is there that the similarity ends!

Sports reporting is filled with opinion, flashbacks, flash-forwards, comparisons, contrasts, reminiscences, exaggeration, punchy verbs, firey language, and word play. Sports reporting — although it often goes without recognition — has produced some of the finest writing to be found in print.

The plan for the sports report usually follows the same plan as the news story. Although the sports report has no place in science or social studies writing, it does provide an excellent summary technique for sports stories connected with reading for English class. Moreover, it's a fine teacher of writing skills.

Model for a Sports Report

Frances Nast thrilled two million fans as she broke out of the pack of 10,000 and through the tape at the finish line to win a marathon miracle in 2 hours and 23 minutes, net! The crowd roared their approval for the twenty-nine-year-old Norwegian-born athlete as she set a new record for herself and a new world record for women runners.

When asked for her comments moments after the computor spelled out the victory greeting in liquid numbers, Ms. Nast, a star-veteran of more than twenty-five marathons, only waited for composure. She poured tepid water over her face and arms;

and, in her friendly style said that runners are super-verbal, but not immediately after a 26 mile and 300 yard run.

Quietly gasping while whiping rivulets of sweat from her eyes, Frances managed to wave encouragement to others coming over the finish line at Central Park's Tavern on the Green.

When asked about the toughest stretch of the run, Ms. Nast said, "That hill up to the Queensborough Bridge. Those seven degrees seemed like seventy at the time."

Ms. Nast also spoke about the charm of the marathon. "I had the impression, even in Staten Island, that I was running through a series of connected, Old World villages. When the gun went off at 10:30 it was like the United Nations. By 11:00, from the faces in the crowd, I figured I was in Finland. By 11:15, the street and shop signs spoke Polska. After that, it was like a world tour."

Ms. Nast suggested the road conditions be improved. She said that there were pot-hole-hazards. Garbage. Sometimes the crowds pushed too far into the street. She also complained that a number of runners slipped and fell on the debris.

On the good side, Ms. Nast identified the New York spectators, especially on Fifth Avenue in Spanish Harlem, as the best crowd in the world.

As for running next year, Ms. Nast replied, "I should defeat my own victory!"

Those of us who have followed Frances-the-fast-Nast from her first breakthrough at Kukora to this sensational triumph of New York City's marathon number seven know that being noncommittal on future runs is part of the Nast style.

However, this is one reporter who will bet on running's golden-girl, Frances-the-fast-est, to not only run in next year's

Big Apple marathon, but to gild her own time. And, I'll

personally be there in the press box, waiting to cheer her over

the finish line.

In this model for sports reporting the language has been fully developed so that you can examine the lengths to which the sports writer might go. Unlike the news report, sports reporting has almost unlimited freedom. Sports writers may interject their personalities — and that includes favoritism and contempt — and show-off their writing expertise.

Showing-off is not the prescribed style for news reporting because any type of word-play, expert or inept, could dangerously color and alter the reality of the event being covered. News writers for news magazines and story magazines do, however, practice the free-style characterized in this model. And, recently, the front page of the *New York Times* has experienced a revolution in free-style writing.

Often, you will hear students and adults say that they liked an article or book for its style. Let the comment go by because most writing has no particularly identifiable style. However, in the model for the sports report, the free-style can be identified by its flippant, zany, made-only-for-the-moment words and word-play.

And a final comment on any type of reporting: always make it easy for the reader to understand.

Both news and sports reporting can contribute an important technique to writing, and that is the *crash-paragraph*. In crash-paragraphing, the writer changes paragraphs without connectives linking one paragraph to the next.

There are special reasons for crash-paragraphing. The writer often has to deal with a variety of facts that resist being properly grouped into cohesive paragraphs. The writer must also deal with multiple quotations, which — as you already learned from *Dialogue* — each get an indentation of their own, and that might include extensive commentary by the writer. Moreover, this quotation requirement makes for a patched-together report. But, considering the tight space limitations in that news and sports reporting isn't written to fit the story, rather it's written to fit the space or the number of column-inches allowed, crash-paragraphing has its practical sides. Too, news and sports reports often get chopped up so that they can fit into smaller than planned spaces. Finally, considering the tight time-frame where news and sports writers are always racing to meet a deadline, crash-paragraphing is simply part of the craft.

For the student who has learned good paragraphing techniques, directions, and how to link one paragraph to the next, the fact that journalism ignores these rules is at first shocking. However, journalism exists to sell newspapers, and, in that sense there is a positive side to crash-paragraphing. It gives the report an easy-to-read look that is welcomed by many. Remember, newspapers have to be sold to the many if they are going to stay in business. Most newspaper readers are in a hurry. They want to know what's going on in the word, but they want to acquire the information with as little effort as possible. ∎

11

The Essay

— Writing is teaching —

W hat is an *essay?*

When we talked about all the various paragraphs, or the technique of dialogue, anecdotes, and short reports, we could get at the rules that governed them. We had a good understanding of exactly what we were working with. However, with the essay, we are going to begin with what it is we do not know.

The essay has no definition.
The essay has no plot.
The essay may or may not have characters.
The essay has no set of governing rules.

Then, what do we know?

We know that the essay does whatever its author wants it to do which may be to mechanically articulate, to babble, to cry out, to dramatize, to entertain, to engineer, to fantasize, to fictionalize, to generalize, to idealize, to joke, to knock, to lament, to lie, to masque, to nourish, to simply observe, to polarize, to quote, to research, to serve, to triumph, to trivialize, to understand, to unify, and to wreck. In any case, the essay is certainly a measure of any writer's expertise, and a work that is often written with much zeal.

Unfortunately, we cannot get at the heart of the essay if we're going to concentrate on all of its many sides.

Cicero, the Roman of classical times who is usually credited with developing the essay, broke the technique into three simple parts which could all be identified by the same word, *tell.* Tell what it is you're going to tell; tell it; then tell that you told it.

This tell-tell-tell formula may sound overly simple to you because you have acquired specialized skills; however, the tell-tell-tell formula will make good sense to you after you have the experience of writing a few essays. Then too, the tell-tell-tell formula is the one sure way to lay out your essay paragraphs, and then, test their validity.

You will want to include these suggestions in essay writing:

Make your essay personal. The best way to do this is by putting a person into the material. Use a real character; or use a fictitious one; and, include yourself.

Make your essay teach. The best way to do this is by reading your way to a knowledgeable position on your topic. You will want to pick up on what might be some of the specialized vocabulary. Know about the current problems, or trends. Know what others are thinking and saying about the topic. Know what the leaders are doing and saying and know who they are and how to spell their names. Take notes and get it straight because your reading is going to become the source of facts for others.

Make your essay thoughtful. After gathering your details and writing them into the chosen paragraph designs, you're going to develop some personal thoughts because of your intense exposure to the material. These opinions are probably going to be strong ones, and they not only belong in your essay, but they will provide it with the strength it needs.

Make your point. These newly acquired thoughts are going to be your point. Always take a powerful stand. Don't tell both sides of the story. Don't try to be fair. Your only goals is to win the readers to your point of view.

There is no better way to grasp the real workings of an essay than through studying one.

The model on page 121 was written by a student who had never before written an essay. He worked from the tell-tell-tell formula. He planned his essay according to the plan on page 120.

The assignment: write a 300-word anti-smoking essay.

Plan for an Essay

Narrative
Tell a story where cigarette smoking turns out to be bad for someone's health.

Exposition
Tell what caused your character to get into smoking.

Persuasion
Based on your reading material, tell why you have made the decision to not smoke.

Abbreviated paragraphs were used to plan this essay. You will note that each of the three paragraphs have been drawn from the paragraphs demonstrated in this book.

Model for an Essay

Sam tried hard to get comfortable. The air conditioner had broken down that afternoon, and now the air in his bedroom was deathly still except that a few sounds drifted up from the almost deserted streets. He tried to pretend that going to sleep wasn't all that important. What could anyone expect him to think on these too-hot-to-handle August nights? So, he punched his pillow into place, flicked on the TV, lit a cigarette, and, half-sitting-up, he waited for the night to pass. At two-thirty a dull-orange glow filled his apartment and gray smoke began funneling from the open windows. Only minutes later fire trucks were screaming through the streets. But it was too late. Sam Howard was already dead.

Sam had just celebrated his thirty-sixth birthday. Of course, his problems didn't really begin on that fateful night. They started about twenty years ago when he was back in high school. At that time it seemed to Sam that there were so many good reasons to smoke. He'd never smoked before, but he liked what he saw in the TV commercials, in the magazines, and on the billboards. Everybody he knew had an opinion about what brand of cigarettes were best. It was a new school and he was making new friends. Since they smoked — and they told him right out that smoking would make him look cool — he started smoking too. Sam thought that smoking made him look older; that it got him friends, the in-kind; and, that the best-looking girls went for guys who smoked. Small wonder Sam never gave a thought to quitting. Smoking became a fixed part of his life-style. He was hooked . . . forever!

In spite of all the arguments in favor of cigarettes, I have made the decision to not smoke. It has taken me some time and heavy thinking, but these are — to me at least — the three main reasons for my decision. The first, and admittedly the most personal, is that people who smoke don't smell good and they don't look good. They look foolish and cheap. The next reason is that smoking two packs of cigarettes a day runs up a bill of about $560 a year: that's $5,000 for ten years; but, that's a whopping $56,000 for life. No wonder the tabacco industry is anxious to get everyone into smoking. However, my last and most important reason for not smoking is that cigarettes can kill. Even light smokers are subject to lung cancer, heart disease, bronchitis, and emphysema. So, I've decided to never start smoking; and, I'd advise you not to either. But, if Sam Howard were around today he would advise everyone against cigarette smoking: the ashes from that mistake just might be your own!

The opening paragraph of this anti-smoking essay uses the *shock-approach*. The narrative begins innocently; it meanders through Sam Howard's difficulty in falling asleep — a problem to which every reader can easily relate — but the actual tragedy is purposefully withheld until the last line of the paragraph.

Note that Sam Howard, through a flash-back technique, carries the reader into the second paragraph and also provides for an exposition on how and why young people are drawn to smoking cigarettes.

The closing paragraph is a paragraph to persuade. Closing that paragraph by returning to Sam Howard provides a powerful and an elliptical ending.

The following model paragraph to open an anti-smoking essay, is also a shock-approach, but with this twist: this is a famous-person approach.

Model for the Famous-Person Approach

The doctors weren't kidding when they told Hollywood's most famous and revered actor — the all-American good-guy — that he had lung cancer. It was disclosed to him, to his family, and to the public that he was suffering from the disease.

He was fighting for his life and decided to try a diet that reportedly makes the body almost perfect. The theory behind the diet is that by eating highly nutritious foods, the body could become so chemically balanced that all cancerous cells would be destroyed. The theory was feasable, but in practice it failed: cancer is sometimes an unreasonable enemy. The actor had to go for extensive surgery. Other complications developed, but cancer was the primary cause of death. What did this tragic end have to do with the fact that John Wayne smoked?

The famous-person approach where you tell a relevant section of the character's history — but you don't reveal the name until the last line — is always a good way to begin an essay or report.

The following model is another useful introduction for an anti-smoking essay. This is also a shock-approach, but with this subtle variation: this narrative does not tell about the character's tragic end; instead, it *shows*.

Model for the Show Approach

Mr. Wilson was sitting at home watching T.V. After slowly crushing hs cigarette into the bottom of the ashtray, he reached for the bottle of pills to ease his pain. Beside his bed stood the oxygen tank, and next to him — so that it was within easy reach, was his mask. Wilson grabbed the mask and placed it over his mouth. He was having trouble breathing. A neighbor walked in, saw that it was an emergency, and called an ambulance. The vehicle arrived quickly and rushed Wilson to the hospital. He was immediately brought to intensive-care where a team struggled to save his life. When the doctors finally came out of I. C. U. they looked like they had bad news. One finally said, "Call the next of kin."

This introduction uses the advanced writing technique of *showing*. Of course, the author told, but in a special way: Mr. Wilson smokes his way into the ambulance; then, instead of allowing even the nameless doctors to use the word death, the author neatly has one say, "Call the next of kin."

Telling by way of showing is a technique that every serious would-be writer will want to master.

The following introductory paragraph to an anti-smoking essay is done in the anecdotal style.
This is the scene: one ghost offers another a cigarette.
This is the caption: "Noooooooo . . . thank you. That's how I got here in the first place."

Model for the Comic Approach

No one knew who he was or where he came from, but it was generally agreed by all the neighbors, that he'd taken permanent residence in the vacant house on East 17th Street. Moreover, although you could see right through him, it was also agreed that he was the image in manner and speech of the former owner, now deceased. The deceased, in his lifetime, had been a gregarious fellow, so it fit in that the ghost on 17th

Street had constant company. Afterall, ghosts can be friendly, too. Then, one afternoon, our resident ghost and a guest were sunning themselves on the patio when cigarettes and a lighter magically appeared. The guest offered a smoke to her host. He replied in tones that made me want to cover my ears. "Nooooooo . . . thank you. That's how I got to be who I am in the first place."

The comic approach to the essay is an entertaining way to enter your discussion. Although all worthwhile introductory paragraphs should have an element of surprise, the comic approach can get double applause because it is made up of both surprise and humor, which in writing is a kind of surprise in itself. Moreover, beginning with comedy, then touching on comedy again at the closing, is an achievement worthy of recognition: it's both skillful thinking and writing to add controlled humor to any well-designed essay.

Any dramatic type of essay such as accidents in the home, forest fires, anti-alcohol or anti-drug themes could profit from an introduction with high shock value.

But, some essays couldn't possibly carry the weight of so dramatic an introduction. What do you do, for example, when the teacher says, "Write an essay on what you did this summer." Or, "Write an essay on your first day back at school."

Let's assume you're going to use the same three-paragraph approach shown on page 120.

Next, you're going to need a theme. Here is a range of emotions any of us might feel in any situation: terror, fear, isolation, rejection, discomfort, comfort, acceptance, security, in-charge, and elation.

Now, let's switch our introductory paragraph from the narrative to a Zig-Zag. Remember, question, connective, your story, connective, and closing sentence from which you can steer your essay.

Model for a Zig-Zag Introduction

Can you remember your first day of high school? I sure can! And it's this one particular instance that sticks in my mind. I had been assigned to an advanced speech class where, judging by the size of everyone around me, they were all in their senior year. The teacher, a smiling woman in a print dress, emphasized that those whose names were not on her list could not remain in her class. She began reading. It was supposed to be a small class, and I wanted very badly to be in it. She called out the names. Those whose names were called answered, and *the rest left. Why she repeated that one name over and over, I*

couldn't figure out. Then, when in exasperation she shouted, I

came to my senses and realized it was the one name I wanted to

hear. My own. I never felt more elated in my life.

The second paragraph of such an essay could be the before and after telling how the author was at the beginning of the year, then shifting to a more mature picture of the author at the end of the year.

The third paragraph of this essay could be a paragraph to convince on why the author felt fortunate to have had this speech class, or this teacher, or been a student in this particular school.

In writing essays, go creative on the introductory paragraph, then let good homework and paragraph design take care of the rest.

The essay is both the workhorse and the thoroughbred of the writer's stable: it's journalism, sports and feature writing, business reporting and public speaking, political campaigning, and even the stuff of which constitutions are made.

However, the essay carries the special weight of responsibility. What goes on paper and into print must pass this test of passage:

The essay must always be built on a good plan;

The essay must always draw from careful study and appropriate language.

The essay must always be the truth.

The essay must state that this author is worthy of publication.

12

Framing Longer Works

— Good writing is success by design —

Whether you are thinking about writing a book report, a paper for social studies, or science, you will be ahead if you build your work on a winning plan. To dream of writing a successful paper without first having a successful plan is like dreaming that one is going to have a successful life without putting down the foundation with which to get it. Dreaming doesn't write successful anything; good planning does!

Let's look at the tools we already have:

You have a knowledge of paragraph plans. With that knowledge you could design whatever type of paragraph you need to present whatever type of material. However, to plan a longer work with a series of paragraph plans is not an appropriate beginning point because the details of the plans will get in your way.

So, let's work with abbreviated paragraphs. This is the symbol we will use.

The abbreviated paragraph symbol helps frame your longer work because it puts first things first: namely, not what you are going to write, but how you are going to write it.

Simple enough: we take the empty paragraph symbol and write in the type of paragraph plan we expect to use.

Narrative

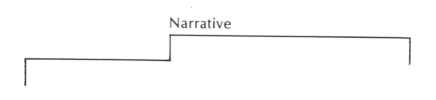

But, we also know that we want this paragraph to introduce a longer work. That's important information to be added.

Narrative Introduction

Now that we have limited our space and style of paragraph, we can concentrate on what it is we want to say.

Narrative Introduction

Tell the story of Aaron Burr's duel with Alexander Hamilton.

We now know the space within which we must work, we know the paragraph style, and we know what material we are going to use. The next question deals with what further controls do we want to use. Let's use a technique with which we are already familiar.

Narrative Introduction

Tell the story of Aaron Burr's duel with Alexander Hamilton.

Famous person approach.

Once we have the refinement of this control, we are ready to set the tone for an entire paper. Here we must ask ourselves how we want to characterize Aaron Burr? As a human being trying to avoid entrapment? As a ruthlessly ambitious politician? As a fool? As a psychotic? As a man acting upon the rules of conduct of his time?

Whatever our choice — and remember it is this choice that is going to become the theme of the paper, the theme about which all the following paragraph discussions will in some way be related — you must include it in this opening.

Narrative Introduction

Tell the story of Aaron Burr's duel with Alexander Hamilton.

Famous person approach.
As a ruthlessly ambitious politician.

You now know how to control a paragraph. Knowing how to control writing is part of framing longer works. Knowing now to control space is important too. At this time, we are going to want to learn how to write in groups of paragraphs or *paragraph sets*. You will want to skip spaces between paragraph sets for the longer work, but you won't want to skip spaces between paragraphs in a set. Sets show that this section of the report centers on a closely related set of details.

This is the symbol for a paragraph set.

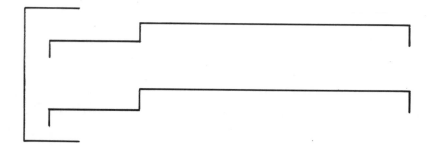

By putting a simple bracket on the left, we know that these paragraphs go together in a set, forming a small discussion within a larger one.

Let's enlarge on a narrative. We might break it into two parts because it's too long for one.

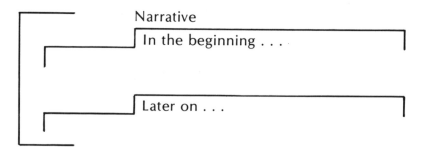

Or, we could expand the narrative to a set of three paragraphs.

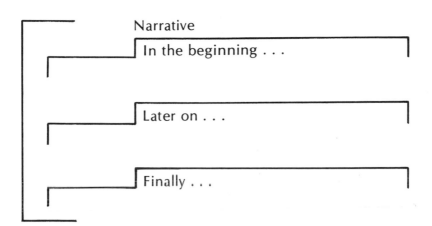

But what would happen if we took this same narrative and recycled it in abstract terms? For example, you want to retell the story-line of a book on which you are reporting. What if you took that story line and recycled it into problem, turning point, and the climax? How might we frame that?

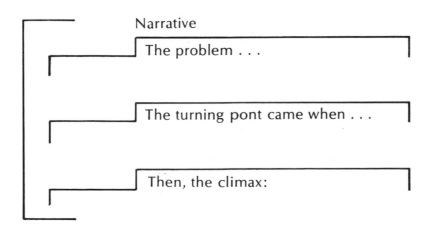

Another abstraction that is always useful for recycling a story-line is conflict. Present your reader with a paragraph set on conflicts arranged in order of importance.

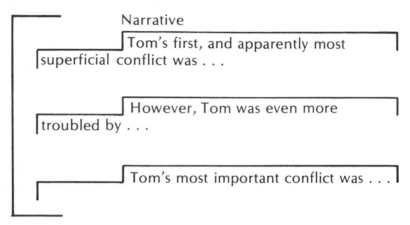

Narrative

Tom's first, and apparently most superficial conflict was . . .

However, Tom was even more troubled by . . .

Tom's most important conflict was . . .

You can also make successful sets for framing the longer paper by splitting some of the paragraph plans you have already learned. For example:

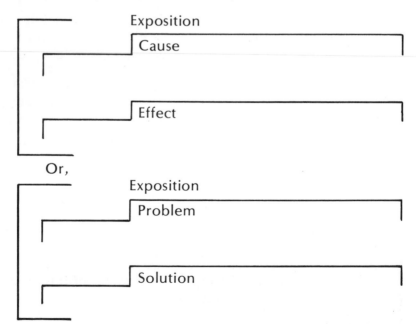

Exposition

Cause

Effect

Or,

Exposition

Problem

Solution

Now that you know something about the use of paragraph sets in framing longer works, we can look at the set for yet another and more personal use: that is the weaving of your observations, experience, and ideas into the writing. To do this, we will want to borrow again from the basic paragraph plans, the paragraph for parallel development.

Let's say you want to discuss a family situation in a novel on which you are reporting for English. And curiously, you have an identical situation within your own family.

Use a paragraph set.

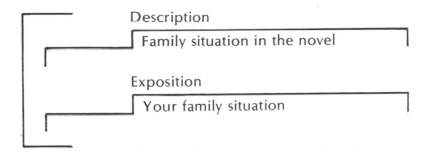

Description

Family situation in the novel

Exposition

Your family situation

Or, you may find it convenient to set up a parallel set by writing about an opposite situation.

Exposition

How a family problem was managed in the novel.

Narrative

How, in your observation, the opposite exists in your community.

Or, you may want to write about material that has a slight or oblique relationship to the material in the novel.

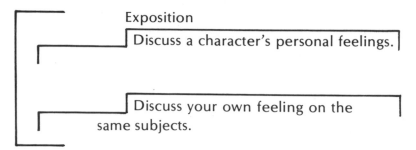

Exposition
Discuss a character's personal feelings.

Discuss your own feeling on the same subjects.

There is an additional step you will want to take in creating paragraphs sets, and that is the technique of *returning*. At the end of the second paragraph in your set, you will find it useful to create a closing sentence that reaches back and reconnects with the material presented in the first paragraph of the set.

Now that you have learned to work with parallels in sets, let's look at yet another application of parallel development. Remember the plan on page 69, and the model on page 70? Let's, for purposes of breaking up the solid-paragraph-look, split it into a three-paragraph set.

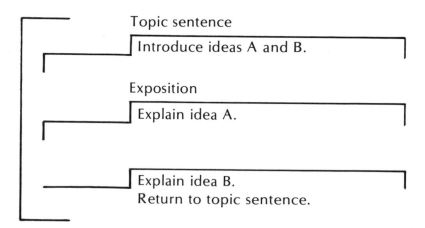

Topic sentence
Introduce ideas A and B.

Exposition
Explain idea A.

Explain idea B.
Return to topic sentence.

Now, we can go on to specific writing projects through the use of the abbreviated paragraph and the paragraph set.

The following framing plans are only suggestions on how to write for English, science, and social studies. You may mix and match however you see your way clear to do so. Remember, the framing for a longer work can always be altered: where you had planned an exposition, you might find the material moving into a narration; or you might find it appropriate to plunk a detailed description into the middle of a narration.   ■

13

How To Write For English

— Writing is the record of human experience—

Framing a Book Report with Emphasis on the Story-line

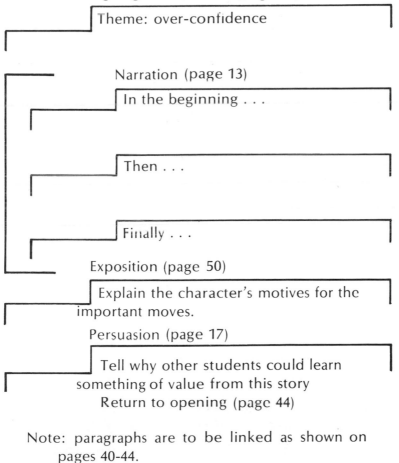

Zig-Zag Introduction (page 21)

Theme: over-confidence

Narration (page 13)

In the beginning . . .

Then . . .

Finally . . .

Exposition (page 50)

Explain the character's motives for the important moves.

Persuasion (page 17)

Tell why other students could learn something of value from this story

Return to opening (page 44)

Note: paragraphs are to be linked as shown on pages 40-44.

Framing a Book Report with Emphasis on Characterization

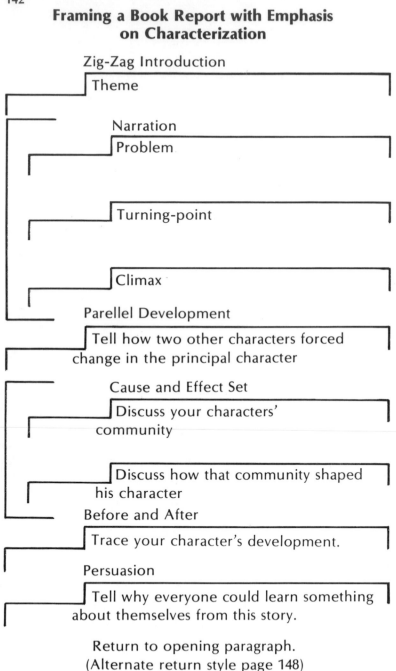

Zig-Zag Introduction

Theme

Narration

Problem

Turning-point

Climax

Parellel Development

Tell how two other characters forced change in the principal character

Cause and Effect Set

Discuss your characters' community

Discuss how that community shaped his character

Before and After

Trace your character's development.

Persuasion

Tell why everyone could learn something about themselves from this story.

Return to opening paragraph.
(Alternate return style page 148)

Note: paragraphs are to be linked as shown on pages 40-44.

Framing a Book Report with Emphasis on Personal and Social Problems

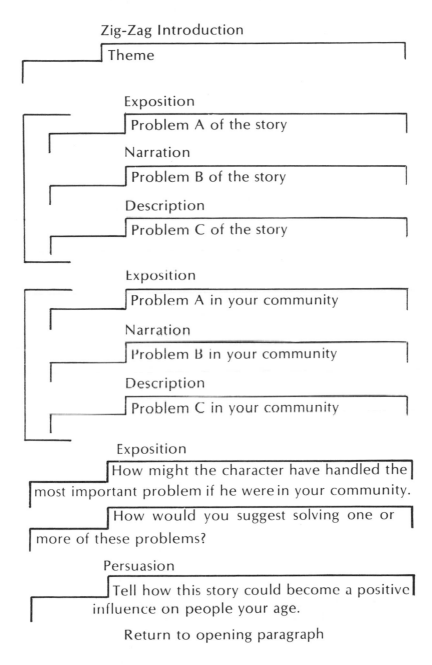

Zig-Zag Introduction

Theme

Exposition

Problem A of the story

Narration

Problem B of the story

Description

Problem C of the story

Exposition

Problem A in your community

Narration

Problem B in your community

Description

Problem C in your community

Exposition

How might the character have handled the most important problem if he were in your community.

How would you suggest solving one or more of these problems?

Persuasion

Tell how this story could become a positive influence on people your age.

Return to opening paragraph

Framing a Book Report with Emphasis on Conflicts

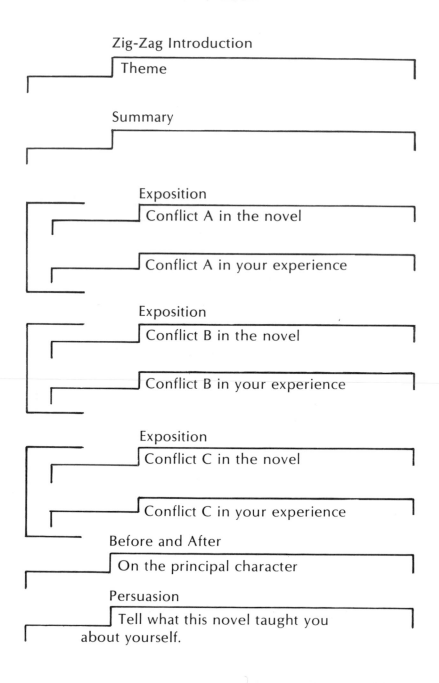

Zig-Zag Introduction

Theme

Summary

Exposition

Conflict A in the novel

Conflict A in your experience

Exposition

Conflict B in the novel

Conflict B in your experience

Exposition

Conflict C in the novel

Conflict C in your experience

Before and After

On the principal character

Persuasion

Tell what this novel taught you about yourself.

Framing a Report on a Biography
with Emphasis on Content

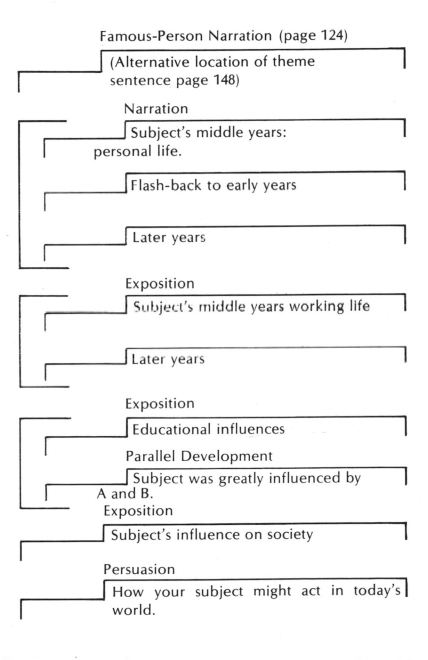

Famous-Person Narration (page 124)

(Alternative location of theme sentence page 148)

Narration

Subject's middle years: personal life.

Flash-back to early years

Later years

Exposition

Subject's middle years working life

Later years

Exposition

Educational influences

Parallel Development

Subject was greatly influenced by A and B.

Exposition

Subject's influence on society

Persuasion

How your subject might act in today's world.

Framing a Report on Biography
with Emphasis on Character

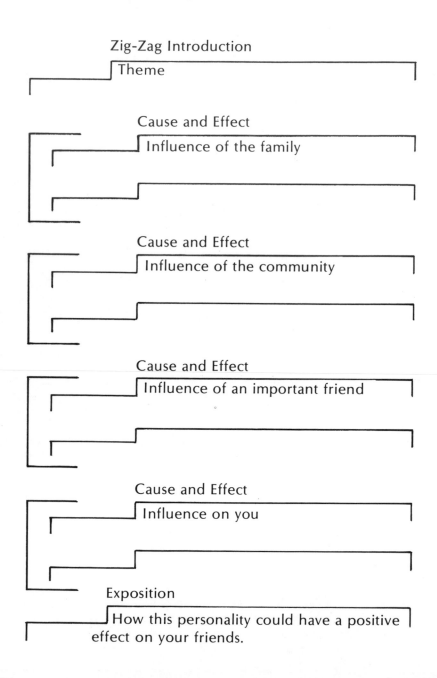

Zig-Zag Introduction

Theme

Cause and Effect

Influence of the family

Cause and Effect

Influence of the community

Cause and Effect

Influence of an important friend

Cause and Effect

Influence on you

Exposition

How this personality could have a positive effect on your friends.

Framing a Report on a Biography with Emphasis on Conflict

Zig-Zag Introduction

Theme

Narration

Early life of subject

Later life

Problem and Solution

Conflict with family

Problem and Solution

Conflict with friends

Problem and Solution

Conflict with tradition

Problem and Solution

Economic problems

Problem and Solution

Primary personal conflict

Exposition

What have you learned about yourself and your life-style from this book? Return to opening paragraph.

Two additional suggestions:

When using any one of the narrative introductions you will want to put your theme sentence into another paragraph so that your opening retains its full effect. And, of course, you'll want to get that theme sentence on your paper as early as possible. I suggest using the theme sentence as an introduction to the second paragraph in your report.

For example:

Such was one dramatic example in Arthur's life as told by Margaret Jackson in her short story, The Stepmother. In the beginning . . .

When ending your report, regardless of what paragraph plan you are using, you're probably going to want to return to your report's opening to achieve an elliptical effect. However, you may find it awkward to add your return to the end of that paragragraph. I suggest then, that you add a one-sentence paragraph to your report: this technique is called *the return.*

For example:

For a compact picture on what over-confidence can do, I recommend that you take a good look at Earnest Thayer's famous poem. "Casey at the Bat."

14

How To Write For Social Studies

— Writing improves the quality of life—

Let's start by borrowing from a report frame with which we are already familiar; namely, reporting on biographies — and that will naturally include autobiographies — as shown in the report frames on pages 145 to 147. You may always write on some famous or not so famous person, and turn out a competent and appropriate report for social studies.

Or, even more appropriately, you might write on the history or development of a community. Unfortunately, there is a certain danger in this chronological perspective: it must be carefully managed if it is going to be kept under control.

However, social studies — independent of the study of history — has developed a reporting style of its own; and, these reports for social studies are right on target when they examine social issues: specifically, as they may be seen in the single individual or the family.

Integrating a family into your report is not as difficult as it might seem at first. What you are going to develop here is a technique for writing a report within a report, and if you borrow from what you have already learned from writing in paragraph sets, this is going to be a natural step.

For example: you decide to allow four paragraphs for this report within a report. The first paragraph, a narrative, might explain how a family arrived and settled in a community. The second paragraph might go on to how they got established, earned their living, traded, and survived or prospered whichever the case might be. The third paragraph might go on to their friends, their relatives, and how they socialized. The last paragraph might describe their education, home, life-style, and religion.

In fact, so inter-related is the individual and the family with social studies reporting that social studies pioneers shaped a specific system of writing for their discipline: this specific, highly specialized system is called *the case study.*

With your training in paragraph plans and framing reports for English, the case study will be a logical step, and will — assuming the quality is there — provide you with unparalleled learning and achieving opportunities in social studies.

Consider this possibility: you are planning a report on your community. More than that you don't know. However, your librarian comes up with material on two families who settled in your community in 1876.

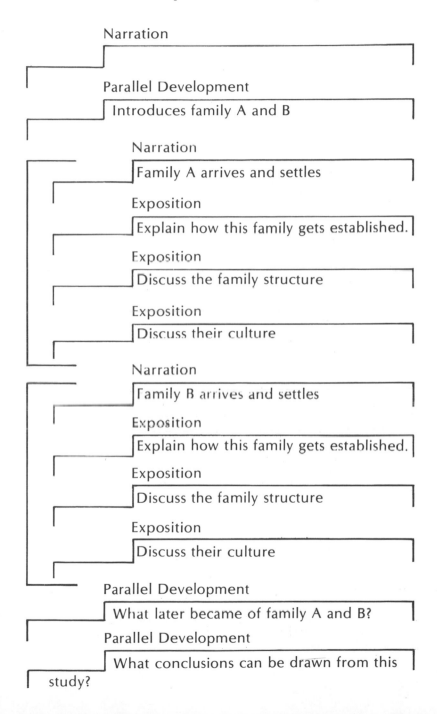

Narration

Parallel Development

Introduces family A and B

Narration

Family A arrives and settles

Exposition

Explain how this family gets established.

Exposition

Discuss the family structure

Exposition

Discuss their culture

Narration

Family B arrives and settles

Exposition

Explain how this family gets established.

Exposition

Discuss the family structure

Exposition

Discuss their culture

Parallel Development

What later became of family A and B?

Parallel Development

What conclusions can be drawn from this study?

Framing a Case Study
with Emphasis on a Given Year

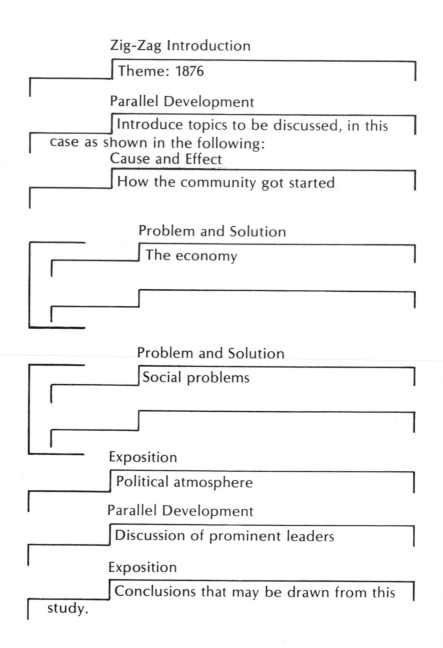

Zig-Zag Introduction

Theme: 1876

Parallel Development

Introduce topics to be discussed, in this case as shown in the following:

Cause and Effect

How the community got started

Problem and Solution

The economy

Problem and Solution

Social problems

Exposition

Political atmosphere

Parallel Development

Discussion of prominent leaders

Exposition

Conclusions that may be drawn from this study.

Framing a Case Study
with Emphasis on a Given Movement

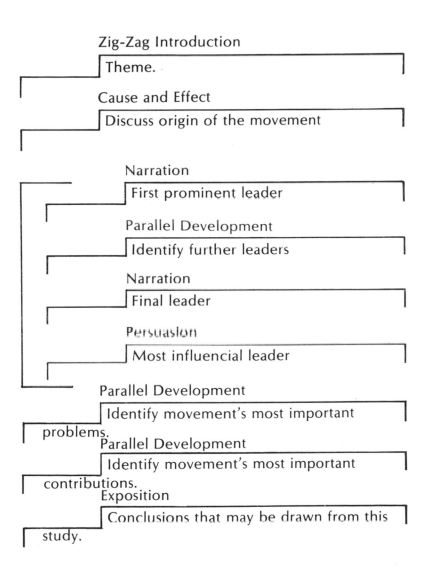

Zig-Zag Introduction

Theme.

Cause and Effect

Discuss origin of the movement

Narration

First prominent leader

Parallel Development

Identify further leaders

Narration

Final leader

Persuasion

Most influencial leader

Parallel Development

Identify movement's most important problems.

Parallel Development

Identify movement's most important contributions.

Exposition

Conclusions that may be drawn from this study.

Framing a Case Study
with Emphasis on a Given Problem

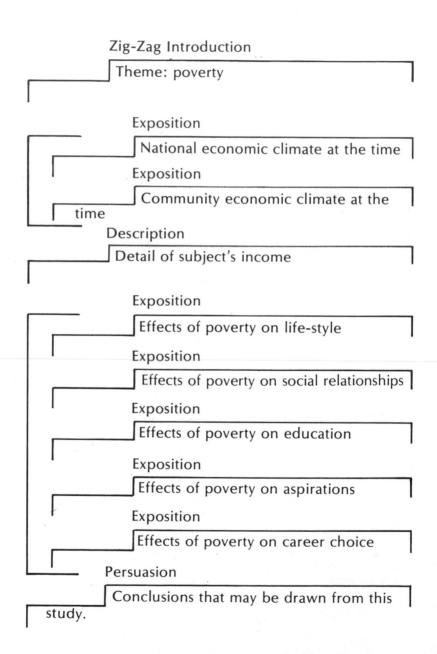

Zig-Zag Introduction

Theme: poverty

Exposition

National economic climate at the time

Exposition

Community economic climate at the time

Description

Detail of subject's income

Exposition

Effects of poverty on life-style

Exposition

Effects of poverty on social relationships

Exposition

Effects of poverty on education

Exposition

Effects of poverty on aspirations

Exposition

Effects of poverty on career choice

Persuasion

Conclusions that may be drawn from this study.

Framing a Study
with Emphasis on a Theme's Variations

Zig-Zag Introduction
Theme: a woman's role, based on characters in a novel or biography.
Exposition
Women in general within that time, culture, and place.
Exposition
Identify a traditional woman

Exposition
Identify the life-style of an apparently dependent woman
Exposition
Identify the life-style of an apparently liberated woman.
Exposition
Identify the characteristics of a woman who has shown considerable growth
Exposition
Women in general within your perspective.

Exposition
The traditional woman

Exposition
The dependent woman

Exposition
The liberated woman

Exposition
The woman who has shown considerable growth
Persuasion
Conclusions that may be drawn from this study.

Framing a Study
Drawn from Multiple Sources

Narration (pages 121-125)

Exposition

Alternative theme position. Introduce
characters from novels or biographies A, B, C, and D.

Exposition

Explain character in source A

Exposition

Explain character in source B

Exposition

Explain character in source C

Exposition

Explain character in source D

Exposition

What generalizations can we draw from this
study?

Persuasion

What criticism might be made on these
diverse presentations?

Exposition

What conclusions might be drawn?

The framing for a study drawn from multiple sources as shown on page 156 is a scaled down version of what is known as the *research paper*. A longer version would simply be an expansion of this study; and a more sophisticated version would be a developmental, expanded version.

Work with this concept of a research paper and you will always be in control: the research paper is a series of diverse discussions related to the central theme.

Writing for social studies offers the student the greatest academic writing activity. Social studies offers unlimited writing material; social studies offers continuously developing problems; social studies material is found in multi-media — TV, films, newspapers, magazines, novels, biographies, drama, radio, personal observation — sources; and, when you write for social studies, you will find that you have very little competition. ∎

15

How To Write For Science

— Writing adds to the common body of knowledge —

$\mathcal{W}$riting for science is possibly your second greatest writing opportunity. And, it's a wide-open opportunity because very few students — including those who seem to excel in science — write for science.

As in English, you might write a report on some famous or not so famous science personality. That is writing a biography; it is *not* science writing.

You might even contact a Nobel Prize winner and put together some first-time-ever material. That is also writing a biography; it is *not* science writing.

Or, you might write an essay on some recent scientific discovery or development; on some current medical advance or environmental problem. You are now within the perameters of science writing.

However, science, like social studies, has carefully developed a specific report system to handle its specialized needs. This special science report was designed to manage the findings of the scientific experiment.

If you are going to present a well-written science report, then you will want to follow the *Framing for a Science Report* on page 161. Moreover, because the science report is a mix of paragraphs, headings and sub-headings, you are going to find it important to follow the step-by-step instructions given on pages 162-164.

There is one additional paragraph that must be explained before one ventures into writing for science, and that is the *abstract*. Curiously, the abstract, which is the first paragraph in the paper, must be written last because it is built up from four sentences: each of these four sentences state a generalization on four parts of the science report; namely, the purpose, the method, the results, and the conclusion. The purpose of the abstract, is to give an up-front summary of the report.

Framing the Science Report

Abstract

Introduction

Exposition

Hypothosis

Exposition

Methods — Type of experiment

Description

Description of the apparatus

Exposition

Explain the results

Exposition

A Discussion

Persuasion

Conclusions drawn from this experiment.

References

1. _____

2. _____

3. _____

Instructions for Presenting the Science Report

If you are going to present a well-written science report, then you will want to set off your material with correct headings, subheadings, and spacing. For best results, follow the instructions step-by-step.

1. Center the *TITLE* of your paper two lines down from the last line in your heading. Underline the title.

2. Skip a line. Center the word *Abstract*. Underline it.

3. Do not skip a line. Indent and write your abstract paragraph. This paragraph consists of four sentences; each sentence describes — in this order — the following: purpose of the experiment, method, generalization of data, and your conclusion.

4. Skip a line. Indent and write your introductory paragraph moving from a generalization on your experiment to a mention of titles of related experiments, to the closing sentence naming your experiment.

5. Skip a line. Center the word *Hypothesis*. Underline it.

6. Do not skip a line. Indent and write your hypothesis sentence. (You may want to have some steering on this from your science teacher.)

7. Skip a line. Center the word *Methods*. Underline it.

8. Do not skip a line. Do not indent. Go all the way to the left-hand margin-line and begin the subheading, *Type of Experiment*. Underline these words.

9. Do not skip a line. Indent and write a paragraph naming and describing the type of experiment you performed.

10. Do not skip a line. Do not indent. Go all the way to the left-hand margin-line and begin the subheading, *Description of Apparatus.* Underline these words.

11. Do not skip a line. Indent and write paragraph to describe your apparatus.

12. Skip a line. Center the word *Results.* Underline it.

13. Do not skip a line. Indent and write as many paragraphs as necessary to discuss all your results. If you plan to include graphs, charts, sketches to show data or comparisons with other experiments, this is the section of your paper in which they belong.

14. Skip a line. Center the word *Discussion.* Underline it.

15. Do not skip a line. Indent and write as many paragraphs as necessary to discuss the experiment; problems you had with it; problems with the materials; problems with the apparatus; how your experiment compares with related experiments; and any additional impressions, tangential ideas, or hunches you might have.

16. Skip a line. Center the word *Conclusions.* Underline it.

17. Do not skip a line. Indent and write a paragraph on your conclusions.

18. Skip a line. Center the word *References.* Underline it.

19. Do not skip a line. Do not indent. Number your references in alphabetical order (see Bibliography on page 171) and enter them 1, 2, 3, each on their own line, as shown on page 174.

20. Each section of this science paper is a separate composition in itself, and each is written at different times. The *Abstract* is written last. It is suggested that you write each of these discussions on a separate sheet of paper; polish the writing to bring it up to the highest standard you can possibly achieve. Then, moving carefully through these instructions, enter your heading, *Title,* each discussion, *subtitles,* and alphabetized references.

If you are looking for essay topics for science writing, you might consider some of the following:

The science of gene-splitting;
the effects of artificial food color and additives on our body;
atomic energy versus fossil fuel energy;
the science of cloning;
diseases of the digestive system;
heart disease, killer number one;
the effects of radiation and drugs on the developing fetus;
the negative effects of marijuana;
alcohol and the body;
psychosomatic illnesses;
where do we go from the space shuttle;
and, the effects of gravity-free conditions on the human body.

Discuss your essay plans with your science teacher before you begin; your teacher may have alternate suggestions.

If you are looking for experiment topics for independent experimentation and science writing, you might want to consider some of the following:

1. *Air Pollution Experiments.* Rutgers, New Brunswick, New Jersey, 1970.

2. Herbert, Don; and Ruchlis, Hy. *Mr. Wizard's 400 Experiments in Science.* Brooklyn, New York. Book-Lab, Inc., 1968.

3. Keen, Martin L. *Let's Experiment.* New York, Grosset and Dunlap, 1976.

4. *700 Science Experiments for Everyone.* UNESCO. New York. Doubleday, 1962.

If you are interested in writing biographical material, you will find a full list of Nobel Prize winners under *AWARDS*, Volume A, *Encyclopedia Britannica.*

16

How To Use The Readers' Guide

— Writing is researching —

Y̊ou have decided to write a paper on *prejudice!*

Now, imagine how you would feel if you went to your social studies teacher for his clearance on your choice of topics; and, instead of giving his stamp of approval he suggests a related, but more controversial topic, *censorship.*

Censorship? You could write a fine paper on prejudice by discussing some of the problems you have observed with your own eyes. But censorship . . . and you wonder where could you possibly get the material.

What your social studies teacher is really telling you is that your original topic is too broad, and that, for a really worthwhile paper you will have to narrow your topic down to a particular area of prejudice. Moreover, censorship would make an excellent topic for a paper if you could get good material. As it happens, you can not only get good material, but all the material that has been printed in the United States in recognized publications within a given time-frame. Your source? *The Readers' Guide to Periodical Literature.*

The Readers' Guide is one of your library's finest reference sources, and your librarian can show you how to use it.

The Readers' Guide is published every month, every six months, and then every year. Go straight to the big, yearly-published volumes. Here's what you'll find on censorship:

CENSORSHIP

Banning books; decision in Island Trees Long Island censorship dispute, A. Neier, Nation 229:390-1 0 27 '79

Book burning in the heartland: Warsaw, Ind. S. Arons. il Sat R 6:24-6+ Same abr. Educ Digest 45:11 D '79

Court upholds Island Trees board in book banning, Long Island, N. Y., M. Reuter Pub W. 216:13 Ag 18 '79

Curriculum censorship in the public school. M. M. Maxson and L. L. Kraus, Educ Digest 45:2-5 N '79

Is academic freedom dead in public schools? L. B. Woods, Phi Delta Kappan, 61:104-6 0, '79

Judge advances fight against Brautigan book ban; Anderson Union High School in Shasta County, Calif. P. Holt Pub W 215:19-20 Ap 9 '79

Ten best censored list: Project Censored list of news stories, Newsweek 94:74 Ag 20 '79

This list is only part of what you will find, but it does represent exactly what you need. Carefully copy or make a Xerox copy of these entries on censorship. Take the list to the librarian in the reference section of your library. It is advisable, in this case, to use your community's largest library. They will have that August 20 issue of *Newsweek*, and those November and December issues of *Educational Digest*. Remember, you can't write on all the recent articles on censorship: these few will do nicely.

Getting material from books to recycle into reports is all right, but books rarely provide the ring of truth, the depth, the accuracy, and the detail. Besides, articles are newer, they are centered on news-making events, they are more relevant because they had a place in the national spotlight, and they are probably more skillfully written.

Should the library not have the issues you need, the librarian will show you how to order reprints.

Use the *Readers' Guide:* it's essential for research because it puts the material you need within your hands.■

17

How To Write A Bibliography

— Writing is giving credit to your sources of material —

*R*eferences—or *Bibliography*—has traditionally been the most troublesome part of student and professional writing.

I think this problem stems from two sources: one, the purpose of the reference section is not clearly understood; and, two — unimaginable as this is going to seem — the author of the paper has to create an abstract of the reference before it can become a part of the *Bibliography*

Let's start with the meaning that references bring to your writing:

References are your credibility: you either fabricated the material yourself, which opens it to considerable question; you stole it, which means that if you would do that you might also be dishonest about what you have written; or your reference sources are not to be respected, which means that what you have written isn't to be respected either.

Then too, references are your credibility because they attest to the level of your source material; they attest to the thoroughness with which you gathered your source materials; they attest—simply by the length of that list—to the high rung on the ladder at which you are beginning your discussion; and finally, your reference listing is your personal responsibility to the writers who have come before you. You will want to give them credit for their contribution just as you will want some future writer to give you credit for the contribution you have made.

And, references are difficult to write because—as the author of the paper—you have to create them before they can take their rightful place within your *Bibliography*.

Here's how the *Bibliography* is done.

First, create the bibliographical abstracts: write down the critical information on each of your sources.

If you used a book with *one author,* you write,

Becker, Carl. *The Declaration of Independence.* New York, Alfred A. Knopf, 1964.

If you drew from a book with *two authors,* you write the names in that order in which they are shown:

Whalen, Frank D. and Parkhill, Wilson. *Our United States.* New York, Noble and Noble, 1956.

If you drew some of your material from an encyclopedia article with an author:

Mandelbaum, David G. "The Colonial Dames of America". Colliers Encyclopedia, 1958.

If you drew some of your material from an *unsigned* encyclopedia article:

"The Five Intolerable Acts", Compton's Pictured Encyclopedia, 1964, Vol XII. Chicago, Ill., Compton, 1964.

If you drew some of your material from an *unsigned* magazine article:

"Are Judges Remaking America?" U.S. News and World Report, December 18, 1967.

If you drew some of your material from a *signed* magazine article:

Moynihan, D.P., "Family Policy for the Nation", America, September 18, 1965.

If you drew some of your material from a book with *three or more authors:*

Chitwood, Oliver Perry and others, The United States from Colonial to World Power, New York, New York, D. Van Nostrand, 1964.

If you drew some of your material from a book where the *editor's name replaced that of the author or authors:*

Langer, William L. ed., An Encyclopedia of World History, Boston, Mass., Houghton, Mifflin, 1962.

If you drew some of your material from a *pamphlet:*

Neal, Fred Warner, *U.S. Foreign Policy and the Soviet Union,* Santa Barbara, Calif., Center for the Study of Democratic Institutions, 1961.

The most difficult part of your *Bibliography* is over; now, to arrange these abstracts in alphabetical order by their first letter. To further clarify the details of this alphabetizing, additional abstracts have been included.

BIBLIOGRAPHY

1. Alden, John Richard. *The American Revolution.* New York, Harper and Row, 1954.

2. Alden, John Richard and Magenis, Alice. *A History of the United States.* New York, American Book Company, 1960.

3. "Are Judges Remaking America?" *U.S. News and World Report,* December 18, 1967.

4. Becker, Carl. *The Declaration of Independence.* New York, Alfred A. Knopf, 1964.

5. "The Five Intolerable Acts". *Compton's Pictured Encyclopedia,* 1964 Vol. XII, Chicago, Ill., Compton, 1964.

6. *John Hancock.* John Hancock Mutual Life Insurance Company, Boston, Mass.

7. Mandelbaum, David G. "The Colonial Dames of America", *Colliers Encyclopedia,* 1958. Vol. V., New York, Colliers and Son, 1958.

8. Moynihan, D.P., "Family Policy for the Nation", *America*, September 18, 1965.

9. Whalen, Frank D. and Parkhill, Wilson, *Our United States*. New York, Noble and Noble, 1953.

And, a closing note: unless you have the capacity to remember every detail—and don't cheat yourself by thinking you can— never try to write a *Bibliography* without using these instructions.　　　　■

18

How To Write Letters

—Writing is managing your affairs—

$\mathcal{T}$here are two types of letters, business and personal. The business letter requires very different skills than other types of writing because it follows a different format, the most troublesome of which is lining up the margins. You will notice that the only indentations in the business letter are in the body.

The business letter requires different thinking skills than those used for any other type of writing because the business letter never says more than it means, and never means more or less that what it says.

The business letter requires superbly crafted sentences.

Business letters fit into categories: there are letters of order, letters of complaint, letters of inquiry, and so on. They all look the same. They are all two-paragraph letters following the problem and solution paragraph set.

When you want to write a business letter, pattern yours after one of the following:

Your home address
City, State Zip

Date

Company to whom you are writing
Address
City, State Zip

Greeting

Problem

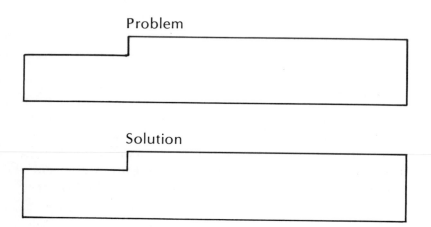

Solution

Closing,

Your Signature

Your Name

Model for a Letter of Request

5201 Scholls Ferry Road
Portland, Oregon 97225

March 18, 19--

Marion County Historical Society
1927 Alder Street
Salem, Oregon 97121

To Whom It May Concern:

As a project for my social studies class I am writing a paper on the early days of Salem.

I would appreciate being sent, to the above address, any free material you have on Salem's early years.

Sincerely,

John Hardworker

Model for a Letter to Order

461 58th Street
Brooklyn, New York 11220

January 21, 19--

The L. and P. Company
Post Office Box 782
Fort Lee, New Jersey 07024

Dear Sir,

    Please send me, at the above address, one navy-blue with white-lettering Rolling Stones Signature T-shirt, size M, as advertised in New York Magazine, January 5, 19--.

    I enclose my personal check for $7.75, which includes postage and handling charges.

Sincerely,

Trendy Thomas

Model for a Letter of Complaint

461 58th Street
Brooklyn, New York 11220

March 4, 19--

The L. and P. Company
Post Office Box 782
Fort Lee, New Jersey 07024

Dear Sir,

On January 21, 19--, I ordered a navy-blue with white-lettering Rolling Stones Signature T-shirt, size M. I enclosed my personal check for $7.75. I am disappointed that the garment sent to me is a Picasso Signature T-shirt, size XL.

I am returning the shirt on this date. Now, I would appreciate your filling my original order, correctly and promptly.

Sincerely,

Trendy Thomas

Letter of Inquiry

813 Grand Avenue
Redlands, California 94590

October 5, 19--

Chairperson, Department of Chemistry
Princeton University
Princeton, New Jersey 07450

To Whom It May Concern:

I am currently seeking information on _____,
who was involved in teaching and research in your department at Princeton, and who recently was awarded the
Nobel Prize in chemistry.

I would appreciate any information you might offer
on _____'s days at Princeton.
Or, you might pass this letter along to someone who knew
_____, was one of his
students, or worked with him. I intend to use the
material in a science project paper.

Sincerely,

Alan Smart

Conclusion

— Good writing is . . .

$\mathcal{N}$ow that you have looked at writing from some of its many sides, you're ready to examine that all-important question: *what is good writing?*

Afterall, if you have conscientiously worked your way through the paragraph system, then you've already taught yourself a great deal about writing; and, naturally, you're going to want feedback on what others think of your work. Meaningful feedback—something you can allow yourself time to think on, in private, yet—would necessarily require several, superbly thought-out, written paragraphs.

Wouldn't this impose an impossible responsibility on your reviewer?

Perhaps, by stepping away from writing, you can easily see how awesome is the task of commenting on someone else's work.

Let's return to the idea of the house. Building a piece of writing is a lot like building a house. And what happens when you bring in outsiders who walk through your work, examining it room by room. Don't assume that the casual critic is in any sense qualified to comment on your achievement! Could the tour have been made with blinders on? How much influence did the neighborhood have? And, in the end, what is there to say? "I liked the colors in the den." Or, "I found a crooked switch-plate in the entrance hall." What comments could these critics make that would be appropriate to the hours you put in, to the subject on which you have written, or to the solid fact that you have produced a product, and . . . they have not?

What then should you expect in the way of feedback?

Written commentary will come only from a *marker*. Markers give grades; they sometimes try to tack on short comments; and they sometimes feel compelled to circle errors in spelling. The most you can hope for is that the marker will find your paper to be the best in the class. Unfortunately, none of this feedback will make you a better writer.

Verbal commentary may also take a variety of styles. There are the *dodgers* who hide, pretending that it is inappropriate to analyze written material. There are the *dreamers* who pretend that good writing may only come as some sudden inspiration. There are the *elitists* who have power to constantly switch views and pretend that good writing is whatever they say it is. There are the *evaders* who will try to sweep you off on some tangent that leads away from your work. There are the *know-nothings* who, at the least, will say nothing; and who, at the most, like to begin with, "I don't pretend to know what good writing is, but I certainly know it when I see it!" And, finally, there are the *name-droppers* who love nothing more than to tell you what they think they know about celebrity writers. None of this feedback will make you a better writer.

Whatever feedback you get saying that your work is good, bad, or indifferent, the commentary is never going to make an in-depth contribution to your writing; however, it is going to make quite an impact on your ego. But, remember, the request for feedback is also a challenge to your critic's ego. Traditionally, the invitation for commentary has been translated into a mandate to find fault. Your reviewers may feel that if they cannot find fault, then they have somehow failed *your* intelligence test. Struggling to win these ego-contests may teach you something about human nature, but nothing about the nature of good writing.

Instead, consider the possibility that you, alone, can achieve good writing.

If you want meaningful feedback on your work, then go the professional writers. Read, read, read; and write, write, write. Make it a high percentage of nonfiction. Constantly compare your work with theirs. Take full responsibility for your priorities: accurately determine what you want to say, your limitations of time and space, your plan, and your personal objective. Take full responsibility for your mechanicals of spelling, punctuating, and clear sentencing. You will become your own best teacher and your own source of meaningful feedback. And then, you will privately understand that . . .

— Good writing is nothing less than

completing each level of the work as you—the

author—have the sole authority so to do —

Index

For bulk orders, special delivery arrangements, for sales representatives opportunities, write
EXCEL PRESS, Box 123, Riverdale, New Jersey 07457.

Please send me **WRITE YOUR WAY TO SUCCESS with The Paragraph System.**
I enclose my check for $12.00.

NAME

ADDRESS

CITY

STATE   ZIP   **EXCEL PRESS**
                                                Box 123
(Allow 4-6 weeks for delivery)   Riverdale, New Jersey 07457

Please send me **WRITE YOUR WAY TO SUCCESS with The Paragraph System.**
I enclose my check for $12.00.

NAME

ADDRESS

CITY

STATE   ZIP   **EXCEL PRESS**
                                                Box 123
(Allow 4-6 weeks for delivery)   Riverdale, New Jersey 07457

Please send me **WRITE YOUR WAY TO SUCCESS with The Paragraph System.**
I enclose my check for $12.00.

NAME

ADDRESS

CITY

STATE   ZIP   **EXCEL PRESS**
                                                Box 123
(Allow 4-6 weeks for delivery)   Riverdale, New Jersey 07457